10th Workshop on Asian Translation 2023 (WAT 2023)

Macau, China
4 September 2023

ISBN: 978-1-7138-9039-3

Printed from e-media with permission by:

Curran Associates, Inc.
57 Morehouse Lane
Red Hook, NY 12571

proceedings.com

Some format issues inherent in the e-media version may also appear in this print version.

Printed with permission by Curran Associates, Inc. (2024)

For permission requests, please contact the Association for Computational Linguistics at the address below.

Association for Computational Linguistics
209 N. Eighth Street
Stroudsburg, Pennsylvania 18360

Phone: 1-570-476-8006
Fax: 1-570-476-0860

acl@aclweb.org

Additional copies of this publication are available from:

Curran Associates, Inc.
57 Morehouse Lane
Red Hook, NY 12571 USA
Phone: 845-758-0400
Fax: 845-758-2633
Email: curran@proceedings.com
Web: www.proceedings.com

WAT 2023

MTS Machine Translation Summit 2023

September 4-8, 2023 Macau SAR, China

Proceedings of the 10th Workshop on Asian Translation (WAT2023)

September 4, 2023

Preface

Many Asian countries are rapidly growing these days and the importance of communicating and exchanging the information with these countries has intensified. To satisfy the demand for communication among these countries, machine translation technology is essential.

Machine translation technology has rapidly evolved recently and it is seeing practical use especially between European languages. However, the translation quality of Asian languages is not that high compared to that of European languages, and machine translation technology for these languages has not reached a stage of proliferation yet. This is not only due to the lack of the language resources for Asian languages but also due to the lack of techniques to correctly transfer the meaning of sentences from/to Asian languages. Consequently, a place for gathering and sharing the resources and knowledge about Asian language translation is necessary to enhance machine translation research for Asian languages.

The Conference on Machine Translation (WMT), the world's largest machine translation workshop, mainly targets on European language. The International Workshop on Spoken Language Translation (IWSLT) has spoken language translation tasks for some Asian languages using TED talk data, but there is no task for written language. The Workshop on Asian Translation (WAT) is an open machine translation evaluation campaign focusing on Asian languages. WAT gathers and shares the resources and knowledge of Asian language translation to understand the problems to be solved for the practical use of machine translation technologies among all Asian countries. WAT is unique in that it is an "open innovation platform": the test data is fixed and open, so participants can repeat evaluations on the same data and confirm changes in translation accuracy over time. WAT has no deadline for the automatic translation quality evaluation (continuous evaluation), so participants can submit translation results at any time.

Following the success of the previous WAT workshops (WAT2014 – WAT2022), WAT2023 will bring together machine translation researchers and users to try, evaluate, share and discuss brand-new ideas about machine translation. For the 10th WAT, we have a Restricted Translation task, Parallel Corpus Filtering task, Multimodal translation tasks, Document-level translation tasks, Indic translation tasks, NICT-SAP tasks, Patent translation tasks, and Non-repetitive Translation task. We had 2 teams participate in the shared tasks. About 40 translation results were submitted to the automatic evaluation server, and selected submissions were manually evaluated. In addition to the shared tasks, WAT2023 also features research papers on topics related to machine translation, especially for Asian languages. The program committee accepted 1 research papers.

We would like to thank all the authors who submitted papers. We also thank the MT-Summit 2023 organizers for their help with administrative matters.

WAT 2023 Organizers

Organizing Committee:

Toshiaki Nakazawa, The University of Tokyo, Japan

Isao Goto, Japan Broadcasting Corporation (NHK), Japan

Hideya Mino, Japan Broadcasting Corporation (NHK), Japan

Kazutaka Kinugawa, Japan Broadcasting Corporation (NHK), Japan

Chenchen Ding, National Institute of Information and Communications Technology (NICT), Japan

Raj Dabre, National Institute of Information and Communications Technology (NICT), Japan

Anoop Kunchukuttan, Microsoft AI and Research, India

Shohei Higashiyama, National Institute of Information and Communications Technology (NICT), Japan

Hiroshi Manabe, National Institute of Information and Communications Technology (NICT), Japan

Shantipriya Parida, Silo AI, Finland

Ondřej Bojar, Charles University, Czech Republic

Chenhui Chu, Kyoto University, Japan

Akiko Eriguchi, Microsoft, USA

Kaori Abe, Tohoku University, Japan

Yusuke Oda, Inspired Cognition, Japan

Makoto Morishita, NTT, Japan

Katsuhito Sudoh, Nara Institute of Science and Technology (NAIST), Japan

Sadao Kurohashi, Kyoto University, Japan

Pushpak Bhattacharyya, Indian Institute of Technology Patna (IITP), India

Technical Collaborators:

Luis Fernando D'Haro, Universidad Politécnica de Madrid, Spain
Rafael E. Banchs, Nanyang Technological University, Singapore
Haizhou Li, National University of Singapore, Singapore
Chen Zhang, National University of Singapore, Singapore

Invited talk: Machine Translation at Wikipedia

Santhosh Thottingal

Wikimedia Foundation

Abstract

Wikipedia, the multilingual encyclopedia available in over 320 languages, uses machine translation technology primarily for article translation. The translation process involves an integrated tool that utilizes various machine translation services to provide initial translations, which are then refined by editors before publication. To date, approximately 1.6 million articles have been translated. This presentation aims to introduce a human-in-the-loop product design, highlighting the provision of high-quality rich text translations through text-only machine translation, coupled with manual curation facilitated by human edits. Additionally, we will share insights and analytics pertaining to translation quality and translators. The discussion will encompass the machine translation engines employed, ranging from free and open-source systems to self-hosted services and external paid APIs. Wikipedia at present has machine translation capability to translate across 198 languages. Lastly, we will present the optimization techniques employed to scale machine translation models in order to meet the performance requirements of Wikipedia.

Biography

Santhosh Thottingal is principal engineer at Wikimedia Foundation Language team. He is based in India. At Wikimedia Foundation, he leads machine translation based projects to fill knowledge gaps in various languages. Santhosh also worked on mediawiki internationalization, technologies that help multilingual speakers to read and write content in wikipedia in their languages. Santhosh is also a typeface designer and known for his fonts for Malayalam script. He was honoured by the President of India in 2019 for his contributions to the Malayalam language.

Table of Contents

Workshop Program

September 4, 2023 [UTC+8]

14:00–14:05 Welcome

Overview of the 10th Workshop on Asian Translation
Toshiaki Nakazawa, Kazutaka Kinugawa, Hideya Mino, Isao Goto, Raj Dabre, Shohei Higashiyama, Shantipriya Parida, Makoto Morishita, Ondřej Bojar, Akiko Eriguchi, Yusuke Oda, Chenhui Chu and Sadao Kurohashi

14:05–14:50 Invited Talk

Machine Translation at Wikipedia
Santhosh Thottingal

14:50–15:10 Research Paper

Mitigating Domain Mismatch in Machine Translation via Paraphrasing
Hyuga Koretaka, Tomoyuki Kajiwara, Atsushi Fujita and Takashi Ninomiya

15:10–16:05 Shared Task

Task Descriptions and Results (Hindi/Malayalam/Bengali Multimodal)
Shantipriya Parida

BITS-P at WAT 2023: Improving Indic Language Multimodal Translation by Image Augmentation using Diffusion Models
Amulya Dash, Hrithik Raj Gupta and Yashvardhan Sharma

OdiaGenAI's Participation at WAT2023
SK Shahid, Guneet Singh Kohli, Sambit Sekhar, Debasish Dhal, Adit Sharma, Shubhendra Khusawash, Shantipriya Parida, Stig-Arne Grönroos and Satya Ranjan Dash

September 4, 2023 [UTC+8] (continued)

16:05–16:10 Closing

Overview of the 10th Workshop on Asian Translation

Toshiaki Nakazawa nakazawa@nlab.ci.i.u-tokyo.ac.jp
The University of Tokyo

Kazutaka Kinugawa kinugawa.k-jg@nhk.or.jp
Hideya Mino mino.h-gq@nhk.or.jp
Isao Goto goto.i-es@nhk.or.jp
NHK

Raj Dabre raj.dabre@nict.go.jp
Shohei Higashiyama shohei.higashiyama@nict.go.jp
National Institute of Information and Communications Technology

Shantipriya Parida shantipriya.parida@silo.ai
Silo AI

Makoto Morishita makoto.morishita@ntt.com
NTT Communication Science Laboratories

Ondřej Bojar bojar@ufal.mff.cuni.cz
Charles University, MFF, ÚFAL

Akiko Eriguchi akikoe@microsoft.com
Microsoft

Yusuke Oda yusuke.oda.c1@tohoku.ac.jp
Tohoku University

Chenhui Chu chu@i.kyoto-u.ac.jp
Sadao Kurohashi kuro@i.kyoto-u.ac.jp
Kyoto University

Abstract

This paper presents the results of the shared tasks from the 10th workshop on Asian translation (WAT2023). For the WAT2023, 2 teams submitted their translation results for the human evaluation. We also accepted 1 research paper. About 40 translation results were submitted to the automatic evaluation server, and selected submissions were manually evaluated.

1 Introduction

The Workshop on Asian Translation (WAT) is an open evaluation campaign focusing on Asian languages. Following the success of the previous workshops WAT2014-WAT2022 Nakazawa

Proceedings of the 10th Workshop on Asian Translation, pages 1–28
September 4, 2023, Macau SAR, China

et al. (2022), WAT2023 brings together machine translation researchers and users to try, evaluate, share and discuss brand-new ideas for machine translation. We have been working toward practical use of machine translation among all Asian countries.

For the 10th WAT, we included the following new tasks/languages:

- Non-Repetitive Translation Task: Japanese $\rightarrow$ English style-controlled translation in the news domain.
- 4 new languages to the Multilingual Indic Machine Translation Task (MultiIndicMT): Sindhi, Santali, Kashmiri, Maithili.

All the tasks are explained in Section 2.

WAT is a unique workshop on Asian language translation with the following characteristics:

- Open innovation platform
  Due to the fixed and open test data, we can repeatedly evaluate translation systems on the same dataset over years. WAT receives submissions at any time; i.e., there is no submission deadline of translation results w.r.t automatic evaluation of translation quality.
- Domain and language pairs
  WAT is the world's first workshop that targets scientific paper domain, and Chinese$\leftrightarrow$Japanese and Korean$\leftrightarrow$Japanese language pairs.
- Evaluation method
  Evaluation is done both automatically and manually. Firstly, all submitted translation results are automatically evaluated using three metrics: BLEU, RIBES and AMFM. Among them, selected translation results are assessed by two kinds of human evaluation: pairwise evaluation and JPO adequacy evaluation.

2 Tasks

2.1 ASPEC+ParaNatCom Task

Traditional ASPEC translation tasks are sentence-level and the translation quality of them seem to be saturated. We think it's high time to move on to document-level evaluation. For the first year, we use ParaNatCom[1] (Parallel English-Japanese abstract corpus made from Nature Communications articles) for the development and test sets of the Document-level Scientific Paper Translation sub-task. We cannot provide document-level training corpus, but you can use ASPEC and any other extra resources.

2.2 Document-level Business Scene Dialogue Translation

There are a lot of ready-to-use parallel corpora for training machine translation systems, however, most of them are in written languages such as web crawl, news-commentary, patents, scientific papers and so on. Even though some of the parallel corpora are in spoken language, they are mostly spoken by only one person (TED talks) or contain a lot of noise (OpenSubtitle). Most of other MT evaluation campaigns adopt the written language, monologue or noisy dialogue parallel corpora for their translation tasks. Traditional ASPEC translation tasks are sentence-level and the translation quality of them seem to be saturated. To move to a highly topical setting of translation of dialogues evaluated at the level of documents, WAT uses BSD Corpus[2] (The Business Scene Dialogue corpus) for the dataset including training, development and test data for the first time this year. Participants of this task must get a copy of BSD corpus by themselves.

[1] http://www2.nict.go.jp/astrec-att/member/mutiyama/paranatcom/

[2] https://github.com/tsuruoka-lab/BSD

Lang	Train	Dev	DevTest	Test-2022	Test-N1	Test-N2	Test-N3	Test-N4
zh-ja	1,000,000	2,000	2,000	10,204	2,000	3,000	204	5,000
ko-ja	1,000,000	2,000	2,000	7,230	2,000	–	230	5,000
en-ja	1,000,000	2,000	2,000	10,668	2,000	3,000	668	5,000

Table 1: Statistics for JPC

2.3 JPC Task

JPO Patent Corpus (JPC) for the patent tasks was constructed by the Japan Patent Office (JPO) in collaboration with NICT. The corpus consists of Chinese-Japanese, Korean-Japanese, and English-Japanese parallel sentences of patent descriptions. Most sentences were extracted from documents with one of four International Patent Classification (IPC) sections: chemistry, electricity, mechanical engineering, and physics. As shown in Table 1, each parallel corpus consists of training, development, development-test, and three or four test datasets. The test datasets have the following characteristics:

- test-2022: the union of the following three sets;
- test-N1: patent documents from patent families published between 2011 and 2013;
- test-N2: patent documents from patent families published between 2016 and 2017;
- test-N3: patent documents published between 2016 and 2017 with manually translated target sentences; and
- test-N4: patent documents from patent families published between 2019 and 2020.

2.4 ALT and UCSY Corpus

The parallel data for Myanmar-English translation tasks at WAT2021 consists of two corpora, the ALT corpus and UCSY corpus.

- The ALT corpus is one part from the Asian Language Treebank (ALT) project Riza et al. (2016), consisting of twenty thousand Myanmar-English parallel sentences from news articles.
- The UCSY corpus Yi Mon Shwe Sin and Khin Mar Soe (2018) is constructed by the NLP Lab, University of Computer Studies, Yangon (UCSY), Myanmar. The corpus consists of 200 thousand Myanmar-English parallel sentences collected from different domains, including news articles and textbooks.

The ALT corpus has been manually segmented into words Ding et al. (2018, 2019), and the UCSY corpus is unsegmented. A script to tokenize the Myanmar data into writing units is released with the data. The automatic evaluation of Myanmar translation results is based on the tokenized writing units, regardless to the segmented words in the ALT data. However, participants can make a use of the segmentation in ALT data in their own manner.

The detailed composition of training, development, and test data of the Myanmar-English translation tasks are listed in Table 2. Notice that both of the corpora have been modified from the data used in WAT2018.

Corpus	Train	Dev	Test
ALT	18,088	1,000	1,018
UCSY	204,539	–	–
All	222,627	1,000	1,018

Table 2: Statistics for the data used in Myanmar-English translation tasks

		Language Pair			
Split	**Domain**	**Hi**	**Id**	**Ms**	**Th**
Train	**ALT**	18,088			
	IT	254,242	158,472	506,739	74,497
Dev	**ALT**	1,000			
	IT	2,016	2,023	2,050	2,049
Test	**ALT**	1,018			
	IT	2,073	2,037	2,050	2,050

Table 3: The NICT-SAP task corpora splits. The corpora belong to two domains: wikinews (ALT) and software documentation (IT). The Wikinews corpora are N-way parallel.

2.5 NICT-SAP Task

In WAT2021, we decided to continue the WAT2020 task for joint multi-domain multilingual neural machine translation involving 4 low-resource Asian languages: Thai (Th), Hindi (Hi), Malay (Ms), Indonesian (Id). English (En) is the source or the target language for the translation directions being evaluated. The purpose of this task was to test the feasibility of multi-domain multilingual solutions for extremely low-resource language pairs and domains. Naturally the solutions could be one-to-many, many-to-one or many-to-many NMT models. The domains in question are Wikinews and IT (specifically, Software Documentation). The total number of evaluation directions are 16 (8 for each domain). There is very little clean and publicly available data for these domains and language pairs and thus we encouraged participants to not only utilize the small Asian Language Treebank (ALT) parallel corpora Thu et al. (2016) but also the parallel corpora from OPUS[3], other WAT tasks (past and present) and WMT[4]. The ALT dataset contains 18,088, 1,000 and 1,018 training, development and testing sentences. As for corpora for the IT domain we only provided evaluation (dev and test sets) corpora[5] Buschbeck and Exel (2020) and encouraged participants to consider GNOME, UBUNTU and KDE corpora from OPUS. We also encouraged the use of monolingual corpora expecting that it would be for pre-trained NMT models such as BART/MBART Lewis et al. (2020); Liu et al. (2020). In Table 3 we give statistics of the aforementioned corpora which we used for the organizer's baselines. Note that the evaluation corpora for both domains are created from documents and thus contain document level meta-data. Participants were encouraged to use document level approaches. Note that we do not exhaustively list[6] all available corpora here and participants were not restricted from using any corpora as long as they are freely available.

[3] `http://opus.nlpl.eu/`
[4] `http://www.statmt.org/wmt20/`
[5] Software Domain Evaluation Splits
[6] `http://lotus.kuee.kyoto-u.ac.jp/WAT/NICT-SAP-Task`

2.6 Structured Document Translation Task

For the first time we introduce a structured document translation task for English ↔ Japanese, Chinese and Korean translation. The goal is to translate sentences with XML annotations in them. The key challenge is to accurately transfer the XML annotations from the marked source language words/phrases to their translations in the target language. The evaluation dataset for this task was created by SAP and is an extension of the software documentation dataset, which is used for the NICT-SAP task. It consists of 2,011 and 2,002 segments in the development and test sets respectively. Note that the dataset also comes with its XML stripped equivalent and can be used to evaluate English ↔ Japanese, Chinese and Korean translation for the software documentation domain. Given that there is no training data available for this task, it becomes more challenging.

2.7 Indic Multilingual Task (MultiIndicMT)

Owing to the increasing interest in Indian language translation and the success of the multilingual Indian languages tasks in 2018 Nakazawa et al. (2018), 2020 Nakazawa et al. (2020a), 2021 Nakazawa et al. (2021b) and 2022 Nakazawa et al. (2022), we decided to enlarge the scope of the 2022 task by adding 4 new languages to the MultiIndicMT task, namely, Santali, Sindhi, Kashmiri and Maithili. In addition to the original 15 Indic languages, alongside English (En), namely, Hindi (Hi), Marathi (Mr), Kannada (Kn), Tamil (Ta), Telugu (Te), Gujarati (Gu), Malayalam (Ml), Bengali (Bn), Oriya (Or), Punjabi (Pa), Assamese (As), Urdu (Ur), Sindhi (Si), Sinhala (Sd) and Nepali (Ne), we have a total of 19 Indic languages being evaluated this year. We used the FLORES-200 dataset's[7] dev and devtest sets for development and testing both containing roughly 1000 sentences each per language. FLORES-200 is N-way parallel which ensures Indic to Indic translation evaluation.

The objective of this task, like the Indic languages tasks in 2018, 2020-2022, is to evaluate the performance of multilingual NMT models for English to Indic and Indic to English translation. The desired solution could be one-to-many, many-to-one or many-to-many NMT models. In general, we encouraged participants to focus on multilingual NMT Dabre et al. (2020) solutions as well as exploiting pre-trained models like IndicBART Dabre et al. (2022) or IndicTrans2 AI4Bharat et al. (2023). For training, we encouraged the use of the Samanantar corpus Ramesh et al. (2022) and its extension, the BPCC corpus AI4Bharat et al. (2023) which covers 18 of the 19 Indic languages. For Sinhala which is not covered by BPCC, we asked users to use the corpora from Opus, specifically the Paracrawl datasets[8]. We also listed additional sources of monolingual corpora for participants to use, namely IndicCorp v2 Doddapaneni et al. (2023).

2.8 English→Hindi Multi-Modal Task

This task is running successfully in WAT since 2019 and attracted many teams working on multimodal machine translation and image captioning in Indian languages Nakazawa et al. (2019, 2020a, 2021a).

For English→Hindi multi-modal translation task, we asked the participants to use Hindi Visual Genome 1.1 corpus (HVG, Parida et al., 2019a,b).[9]

The statistics of HVG 1.1 are given in Table 4. One "item" in HVG consists of an image with a rectangular region highlighting a part of the image, the original English caption of this region and the Hindi reference translation. Depending on the track (see 2.8.1 below), some of these item components are available as the source and some serve as the reference or play the role of a competing candidate solution.

[7] `https://github.com/facebookresearch/flores`

[8] `https://opus.nlpl.eu/ParaCrawl.php`

[9] `https://lindat.mff.cuni.cz/repository/xmlui/handle/11234/1-3267`

Dataset	Items	Tokens English	Tokens Hindi
Training Set	28,930	143,164	145,448
D-Test	998	4,922	4,978
E-Test (EV)	1,595	7,853	7,852
C-Test (CH)	1,400	8,186	8,639

Table 4: Statistics of Hindi Visual Genome 1.1 used for the English→Hindi Multi-Modal translation task. One item consists of a source English sentence, target Hindi sentence, and a rectangular region within an image. The total number of English and Hindi tokens in the dataset also listed. The abbreviations EV and CH are used in the official task names in WAT scoring tables.

	Text-Only MT	**Hindi Captioning**	**Multi-Modal MT**
Image	–		
Source Text	The woman is waiting to cross the street	–	A blue wall beside tennis court
System Output	महिला सड़क पार करने का इंतजार कर रही है	सड़क पर कार	टेनिस कोर्ट के बगल में एक नीली दीवार
Gloss	Woman waiting to cross the street	Car on the road	a blue wall next to the tennis court
Reference Solution	एक महिला सड़क पार करने के लिए इंतजार कर रही है	सड़क के किनारे खड़ी कारें	टेनिस कोर्ट के बगल में एक नीली दीवार
Gloss	the woman is waiting to cross the street	Cars parked along the side of the road	A blue wall beside the tennis court

Figure 1: An illustration of the three tracks of WAT 2023 English→Hindi Multi-Modal Task.

2.8.1 English→Hindi Multi-Modal Task Tracks

1. Text-Only Translation (labeled "TEXT" in WAT official tables): The participants are asked to translate short English captions (text) into Hindi. No visual information can be used. On the other hand, additional text resources are permitted (but they need to be specified in the corresponding system description paper).

2. Hindi Captioning (labeled "HI"): The participants are asked to generate captions in Hindi for the given rectangular region in an input image.

3. Multi-Modal Translation (labeled "MM"): Given an image, a rectangular region in it and an English caption for the rectangular region, the participants are asked to translate the English text into Hindi. Both textual and visual information can be used.

The English→Hindi multi-modal task includes three tracks as illustrated in Figure 1.

English Text: Two elephants standing in the water.

Malayalam Text: വെള്ളത്തിൽ നിൽക്കുന്ന രണ്ട് ആനകൾ

Figure 2: Sample item from Malayalam Visual Genome (MVG), Image with specific region and its description.

2.9 English→Malayalam Multi-Modal Task

This task was introduced in WAT2021 using the first multi-modal machine translation dataset in *Malayalam* language. For English→Malayalam multi-modal translation task we asked the participants to use the Malayalam Visual Genome corpus (MVG for short Parida and Bojar, 2021).[10]

The statistics of MVG are given in Table 5. As in Hindi Visual Genome (see Section 2.8), one "item" in MVG consists of an image with a rectangular region highlighting a part of the image, the original English caption of this region and the Malayalam reference translation as shown in Figure 2. Depending on the track (see 2.9.1 below), some of these item components are available as the source and some serve as the reference or play the role of a competing candidate solution.

2.9.1 English→Malayalam Multi-Modal Task Tracks

1. Text-Only Translation (labeled "TEXT" in WAT official tables): The participants are asked to translate short English captions (text) into Malayalam. No visual information can be used. On the other hand, additional text resources are permitted (but they need to be specified in the corresponding system description paper).

2. Malayalam Captioning (labeled "ML"): The participants are asked to generate captions in Malayalam for the given rectangular region in an input image.

3. Multi-Modal Translation (labeled "MM"): Given an image, a rectangular region in it and an English caption for the rectangular region, the participants are asked to translate the English text into Malayalam. Both textual and visual information can be used.

2.10 English→Bengali Multi-Modal Task

This new task, introduced in WAT2022, uses a multimodal machine translation dataset in *Bengali* language. The task mimics the structure of English→Hindi (Section 2.8) and English→Malayalam (Section 2.9) multi-modal tasks. For English→Bengali multi-modal trans-

[10]https://lindat.mff.cuni.cz/repository/xmlui/handle/11234/1-3533

Dataset	Items	Tokens	
		English	Malayalam
Training Set	28,930	143,112	107,126
D-Test	998	4,922	3,619
E-Test (EV)	1,595	7,853	6,689
C-Test (CH)	1,400	8,186	6,044

Table 5: Statistics of Malayalam Visual Genome used for the English→Malayalam Multi-Modal translation task. One item consists of a source English sentence, target Hindi sentence, and a rectangular region within an image. The total number of English and Malayalam tokens in the dataset also listed. The abbreviations EV and CH are used in the official task names in WAT scoring tables.

English Text: The sharp bird talon.
Bengali Text: ধারালো পাখি টালন

Figure 3: Sample item from Bengali Visual Genome (BVG), Image with a specific region and its description.

lation task we asked the participants to use the Bengali Visual Genome corpus (BVG for short, Sen et al., 2022).[11]

The statistics of BVG are given in Table 6. One "item" in BVG again consists of an image with a rectangular region highlighting a part of the image, the original English caption of this region and the Bengali reference translation as shown in Figure 3. Depending on the track (see Section 2.10.1 below), some of these item components are available as the source and some serve as the reference or play the role of a competing candidate solution.

2.10.1 English→Bengali Multi-Modal Task Tracks

1. Text-Only Translation (labeled "TEXT" in WAT official tables): The participants are asked to translate short English captions (text) into Bengali. No visual information can be used. On the other hand, additional text resources are permitted (but they need to be specified in the corresponding system description paper).

2. Bengali Captioning (labeled "BN"): The participants are asked to generate captions in Ben-

[11] `https://lindat.mff.cuni.cz/repository/xmlui/handle/11234/1-3722`

Dataset	Items	Tokens English	Tokens Bengali
Training Set	28,930	143,115	113,978
D-Test	998	4,922	3,936
E-Test (EV)	1,595	7,853	6,408
C-Test (CH)	1,400	8,186	6,657

Table 6: Statistics of Bengali Visual Genome used for the English→Bengali Multi-Modal translation task. One item consists of a source English sentence, target Bengali sentence, and a rectangular region within an image. The total number of English and Bengali tokens in the dataset also listed. The abbreviations EV and CH are used in the official task names in WAT scoring tables.

gali for the given rectangular region in an input image.

3. Multi-Modal Translation (labeled "MM"): Given an image, a rectangular region in it and an English caption for the rectangular region, the participants are asked to translate the English text into Bengali. Both textual and visual information can be used.

2.11 Ambiguous MS COCO Japanese↔English Multimodal Task

This is the 3rd year that we have organized this task. We provide the Japanese–English Ambiguous MS COCO dataset Merritt et al. (2020) for validation and testing, which contains ambiguous verbs that may require visual information in images for disambiguation. The validation and testing sets contain 230 and 231 Japanese–English sentence pairs, respectively. The Japanese sentences are translated from the English sentences in the original Ambiguous MS COCO dataset.[12]

Participants can use the constrained and unconstrained training data to train their multimodal machine translation system. In the constrained setting, only the Flickr30kEntities Japanese (F30kEnt-Jp) dataset[13] can be used as training data. In the unconstrained setting, the MS COCO English data[14] and STAIR Japanese image captions[15] can be used as additional training data.

We prepare a baseline using the double attention on image region method following Zhao et al. (2020) for both Japanese→English and English→Japanese directions.

2.12 Japanese→English Video Guided MT Task for Ambiguous Subtitles

This is the 2nd year that we have organized this task. We provide VISA Li et al. (2022), an ambiguous subtitles dataset, including $35,880$, $2,000$, and $2,000$ samples for training, validation, and testing, respectively. The dataset contains parallel subtitles in which the Japanese source subtitles are ambiguous and may require visual information in corresponding video clips for disambiguation. Furthermore, according to the cause of ambiguity, the dataset is divided into Polysemy and Omission.

Participants can use the constrained and unconstrained training data to train their multimodal machine translation system. In the constrained setting, only the VISA dataset[16] can be used as training data. In the unconstrained setting, pre-trained models, additional data from other sources can be used as additional training sources.

[12] http://www.statmt.org/wmt17/multimodal-task.html
[13] https://github.com/nlab-mpg/Flickr30kEnt-JP
[14] https://cocodataset.org/#captions-2015
[15] https://stair-lab-cit.github.io/STAIR-captions-web/
[16] https://github.com/ku-nlp/VISA

We prepare a baseline using the spatial hierarchical attention network following Gu et al. (2021) with both motion and spatial features.

2.13 Low-Resource Khmer→English/French Speech Translation Task

This is the 2nd year that we have organized this task. The purpose of this task is to identify effective techniques for speech translation of Khmer into English and French. We expect that the low-resource nature of Khmer will pose a reasonable challenge. To this end, we have curated a dataset from the ECCC corpus Soky et al. (2021), which is an international court dataset consisting of text and speech in Khmer, English, and French. The dataset used for WAT 2023 contains $11,563$, 624, and 626 utterances for training, validation, and testing, respectively. This dataset has a wide range of speakers: witnesses, defendants, judges, clerks or officers, co-prosecutors, experts, defense counsels, civil parties, and interpreters.

Participants can use the constrained and unconstrained training data to train their speech machine translation system. In the constrained setting, only the provided ECCC dataset[17] can be used as training data. Additionally, participants may use pre-trained models such as BART, mBART, mT5, and wav2vec 2.0 as applicable. In the unconstrained setting, additional data from other sources can also be used.

We prepare a baseline using the transformer-based model presented in Soky et al. (2021) for both Khmer→English and Khmer→French directions.

2.14 Restricted Translation Task

Despite recent success of NMT, the MT systems still struggle to generate translation with a consistent terminology. Consistency is the key to clear and accurate translation, especially when translating documents in a specific field, for instance, science or business and marketing contexts, requiring technical terms and proper nouns to get translated into the corresponding unique expressions continuously in the entire documents. To tackle this inconsistent translation issue, we have introduced *Restricted Translation task* since WAT 2021 Nakazawa et al. (2021c).

In this task, participants are required to submit a system that translates source texts under given constraints about the target vocabulary. At inference time, vocabulary constraints are provided as a list of target words and phrases, consisting of scientific technical terms in the target language. The system outputs must contain all these target words. There exist English↔Japanese tasks and Chinese↔Japanese tasks. We employ the ASPEC corpus for all the translation tasks and allow participants to use any other external data sources.

2.15 Parallel Corpus Filtering Task

Machine translation systems are trained from usually large corpora obtained from noisy data sources. Noisy examples in the training corpora are known as the main cause of reducing the translation accuracy of the resulting models Khayrallah and Koehn (2018), and this problem can be mitigated by corpus filtering Koehn et al. (2020), which removes problematic examples from the training corpus, so that the model is eventually trained by cleaner dataset than the data source.

The motivation for this task is inspired by the Parallel Corpus Filtering Tasks held in 2018, 2019, and 2020 Workshop on Machine Translation Koehn et al. (2020), in which the participants are asked to filter the web-crawled corpora, train the NMT model on the cleaner subsets, and evaluate its quality on a multi-domain test set.

This task lets the participants train machine translation models under the following restrictions:

[17] `https://github.com/ksoky/ECCC_DATASET`

Dataset	# sentences
JParaCrawl v3.0	25.7M
WMT22 generaltest2022.en-ja	2,037
WMT22 generaltest2022.ja-en	2,008

Table 7: Number of sentence pairs in the corpora used in the parallel corpus filtering task.

- The model architecture is fixed. The training program is provided as a fixed Docker image by the organizer, and participants can only run a specific training command to build their own model. The same image is used in the final evaluation.
- Training corpus is fixed. The organizer provides the whole corpus, and participants are requested to rank sentences in the corpus by their quality.
- The model will be trained with high-scored sentences (top 100k, 1M, and 10M sentences), and evaluate their translation performance.
- For evaluation, we used WMT22 General Translation Task test-set Kocmi et al. (2022), which includes various domains. Thus domain adaptation by selecting training data is not our scope.

We adopted the Transformer model as the shared architecture for this task.[18] We asked the participants to select a subset from JParaCrawl Morishita et al. (2020), the noisy English-Japanese web-crawled parallel corpus, based on its cleanliness. The baseline model is obtained by training the model on the whole set of this dataset.

We trained the model with the submitted data for both English-Japanese and English-Japanese. We evaluated the submission on both BLEU score Papineni et al. (2002a) and JPO adequacy as described in Section 6.1 on the WMT22 General Translation Task test-set. The corpus statistics are summarized in Table 7.

The ultimate goal of this shared task is to create a cleaner JParaCrawl corpus. After this shared task ends, we plan to ensemble all participant scores and make a cleaner corpus.

2.16 Non-Repetitive Translation Task

We introduce a novel non-repetitive translation task for Japanese → English sentence-level translation. The underlying motivation is to guide a machine translation (MT) system to follow the writing style of the English news domain. To realize high-quality text, English news has many rules, such as using the active rather than the passive voice, using the affirmative rather than the negative, and avoiding redundant phrases (Block, 1994; Cappon, 2019; Papper, 2021). Our goal is to produce high-quality translations that follow a set of writing rules used by professional news translators. For the first year, we focus on the repetition of words or phrases. Here is an example:

(Ja) 入学$_{(1)}$ 予定者７人が教育方針や私立小への入学$_{(2)}$ などを理由に入学$_{(3)}$ を辞退した。

(En) ..., seven children dropped plans to enter the school$_{(3)}$, with parents citing disagreements with its education policy, decisions to join$_{(2)}$ private schools or other reasons, ...

[18]The Dockerfile for constructing the training pipeline can be obtained from https://github.com/MorinoseiMorizo/wat2022-filtering

In this sentence pair, "入学$_{(1)}$" has been intentionally removed in the translation, probably because it is contextually obvious (*reduction*).[19] In addition, "入学$_{(2)}$" and "入学$_{(3)}$" are translated differently as "join$_{(2)}$" and "enter$_{(3)}$," respectively (*substitution*). Unlike technical terms, common words and phrases that are repeated in a sentence can create a monotonous or awkward impression, and should be avoided where appropriate. In this task, participants are required to control an MT system in applying reduction or substitution so that it does not output the same words/phrases for certain repeated words/phrases in the source sentence. We refer to such translations as *non-repetitive translations*. The key point of this task is to control lexical redundancy and diversity while maintaining an accurate translation.

We provide development and test sets containing 70 and 173 examples, respectively. In each set, about one-third of the examples are reductions and the remaining two-thirds are substitutions. This evaluation dataset was constructed from Jiji news articles. In each example, the Japanese source sentence contains one type of repeated word/phrase that is translated with reduction or substitution into the English reference sentence. No training set has been prepared specifically for this task. Although we also provide the dataset including 200K training sentence pairs from the WAT2020 Newswire tasks (Nakazawa et al., 2020b),[20] which was also constructed from Jiji news articles, participants can use any data for training as long as it does not contain the test set in this task. Note that the evaluation dataset for this task partially overlaps with that of the WAT2020 Newswire tasks (Nakazawa et al., 2020b).

To verify that the reductions and substitutions are appropriate, a two-step manual inspection is used instead of automatic metrics. First, three human annotators check the output for mistranslations, undertranslations, or overtranslations, and assign a 0/1 acceptability score to each output. Here, we stress to the annotators that they should be aware of the difference between reduction (removing contextually obvious words/phrases) and undertranslation (failing to output necessary words/phrases). Unacceptable outputs in this stage do not affect the final result. Next, the annotators check whether the target words/phrases have been successfully substituted or reduced, and judge whether the outputs are written in either non-repetitive style or repetitive style. Although an MT system must choose either substitution or reduction to produce a non-repetitive translation style, the choice does not have to be consistent with the reference translation. In addition, the MT system does not necessarily have to choose the same word/phrase as that used in the reference. The final decisions on acceptability and translation style are made by a majority vote of the three annotators at each stage. The reference translation is not shown to the annotators in either evaluation step. The final result is determined by the number of translations that are both acceptable and non-repetitive.

As a baseline, we use the vanilla "big" Ja→En Transformer model (Vaswani et al., 2017) pre-trained on JparaCrawl v3.0 (Morishita et al., 2022), which was downloaded from the authors' website.[21]

3 Participants

Table 8 shows the participants in WAT2023. Both teams participated the Indic Multimodal Tasks. About 40 translation results by 2 teams were submitted for automatic evaluation.

[19] *Reduction* includes sharing a noun head, e.g., "the reopened school and provisional school" → "the reopened and provisional schools."

[20] `https://lotus.kuee.kyoto-u.ac.jp/WAT/jiji-corpus/2020/TaskDescription.html`

[21] `https://www.kecl.ntt.co.jp/icl/lirg/jparacrawl/`

Team ID	Organization	Country
ODIAGEN	Odia Generative AI	India
BITS-P	Birla Institute of Technology and Science, Pilani	India

Table 8: List of participants who submitted translations for the human evaluation in WAT2023

4 Baseline Systems

Human evaluations of most of WAT tasks were conducted as pairwise comparisons between the translation results for a specific baseline system and translation results for each participant's system. That is, the specific baseline system served as the standard for human evaluation. At WAT 2023, we adopted some of neural machine translation (NMT) as baseline systems. The details of the NMT baseline systems are described in this section.

The NMT baseline systems consisted of publicly available software, and the procedures for building the systems and for translating using the systems were published on the WAT web page. We also have SMT baseline systems for the tasks that started at WAT 2017 or before 2017. SMT baseline systems are described in the WAT 2017 overview paper Nakazawa et al. (2017). The commercial RBMT systems and the online translation systems were operated by the organizers. We note that these RBMT companies and online translation companies did not submit their systems. Because our objective is not to compare commercial RBMT systems or online translation systems from companies that did not themselves participate, the system IDs of these systems are anonymous in this paper.

4.1 Tokenization

We used the following tools for tokenization.

4.1.1 For ASPEC, JPC, and ALT+UCSY

- Juman version 7.0[22] for Japanese segmentation.
- Stanford Word Segmenter version 2014-01-04[23] (Chinese Penn Treebank (CTB) model) for Chinese segmentation.
- The Moses toolkit for English and Indonesian tokenization.
- Mecab-ko[24] for Korean segmentation.
- Indic NLP Library[25] Kunchukuttan (2020) for Indic language segmentation.
- The tools included in the ALT corpus for Myanmar and Khmer segmentation.
- subword-nmt[26] for all languages.

When we built BPE-codes, we merged source and target sentences and we used 100,000 for -s option. We used 10 for vocabulary-threshold when subword-nmt applied BPE.

4.1.2 For Indic and NICT-SAP Tasks

- For the Indic task we did not perform any explicit tokenization of the raw data.

- For the NICT-SAP task we only character segmented the Thai corpora as it was the only language for which character level BLEU was to be computed. Other languages corpora were not preprocessed in any way.

[22]http://nlp.ist.i.kyoto-u.ac.jp/EN/index.php?JUMAN

[23]http://nlp.stanford.edu/software/segmenter.shtml

[24]https://bitbucket.org/eunjeon/mecab-ko/

[25]https://github.com/anoopkunchukuttan/indic_nlp_library

[26]https://github.com/rsennrich/subword-nmt

- Any subword segmentation or tokenization was handled by the internal mechanisms of tensor2tensor.

4.1.3 For Structured Document Translation Task

- No tokenization was explicitly performed.

4.1.4 For English→Hindi, English→Malayalam, and English→Bengali Multi-Modal Tasks

- Hindi Visual Genome 1.1, Malayalam Visual Genome, and Bengali Visual Genome come untokenized and we did not use or recommend any specific external tokenizer.

- The standard OpenNMT-py sub-word segmentation was used for pre/post-processing for the baseline system and each participant used what they wanted.

4.1.5 For English↔Japanese Multi-Modal Tasks

- For English sentences, we applied lowercase, punctuation normalization, and the Moses tokenizer.

- For Japanese sentences, we used KyTea for word segmentation.

4.2 Baseline NMT Methods

We used the NMT models for all tasks. Unless mentioned otherwise we use the Transformer model Vaswani et al. (2017). We used OpenNMT Klein et al. (2017) (RNN-model) for ASPEC, JPC, and ALT tasks, tensor2tensor[27] for the NICT-SAP task, HuggingFace transformers[28] for the Structured Document Translation task and OpenNMT-py[29] for other tasks.

4.2.1 NMT with Attention (OpenNMT)

For ASPEC, JPC, and ALT tasks, we used OpenNMT Klein et al. (2017) as the implementation of the baseline NMT systems of NMT with attention (System ID: NMT). We used the following OpenNMT configuration.

- encoder_type = brnn
- brnn_merge = concat
- src_seq_length = 150
- tgt_seq_length = 150
- src_vocab_size = 100000
- tgt_vocab_size = 100000
- src_words_min_frequency = 1
- tgt_words_min_frequency = 1

The default values were used for the other system parameters.

We used the following data for training the NMT baseline systems of NMT with attention.

- All of the training data mentioned in Section 2 were used for training except for the ASPEC Japanese–English task. For the ASPEC Japanese–English task, we only used train-1.txt, which consists of one million parallel sentence pairs with high similarity scores.
- All of the development data for each task was used for validation.

[27] https://github.com/tensorflow/tensor2tensor

[28] https://github.com/huggingface/transformers

[29] https://github.com/OpenNMT/OpenNMT-py

4.2.2 Transformer (Tensor2Tensor)

For the News Commentary task, we used tensor2tensor's[30] implementation of the Transformer Vaswani et al. (2017) and used default hyperparameter settings corresponding to the "base" model for all baseline models. The baseline for the News Commentary task is a multilingual model as described in Imankulova et al. (2019) which is trained using only the in-domain parallel corpora. We use the token trick proposed by Johnson et al. (2017) to train the multilingual model.

For the NICT-SAP task, we used tensor2tensor to train many-to-one and one-to-many models where the latter were trained with the aforementioned token trick. We trained models for all languages except Vietnamese. We used default hyperparameter settings corresponding to the "big" model. Since the NICT-SAP task involves two domains for evaluation (Wikinews and IT) we used a modification of the token trick technique for domain adaptation to distinguish between corpora for different domains. In our case we used tokens such as $2alt$ and $2it$ to indicate whether the sentences belonged to the Wikinews or IT domain, respectively. For both tasks we used 32,000 separate sub-word vocabularies. We trained our models on 1 GPU till convergence on the development set BLEU scores, averaged the last 10 checkpoints (separated by 1000 batches) and performed decoding with a beam of size 4 and a length penalty of 0.6.

4.2.3 Transformer (HuggingFace)

For the Structured Document Translation task, we used the official mbart-50 model fine-tuned[31] for machine translation to directly translate the test sets. We used the HuggingFace transformers implementation to decode sentences using a beam of size 4 and length penalty of 1.0. The tokenization was handled by the mbart-50 tokenizer. Surprisingly, this naive approach actually yielded good results.

4.2.4 Transformer (OpenNMT-py)

For the English→Hindi, English→Malayalam, and English→Bengali Multimodal tasks we used the Transformer model Vaswani et al. (2018) as implemented in OpenNMT-py Klein et al. (2017) and used the "base" model with default parameters for the multi-modal task baseline. We have generated the vocabulary of 32k sub-word types jointly for both the source and target languages. The vocabulary is shared between the encoder and decoder.

5 Automatic Evaluation

5.1 Procedure for Calculating Automatic Evaluation Score

We evaluated translation results by three metrics: BLEU Papineni et al. (2002a), RIBES Isozaki et al. (2010) and AMFM Banchs et al. (2015a). BLEU scores were calculated using SacreBLEU Post (2018). RIBES scores were calculated using `RIBES.py` version 1.02.4.[32] AMFM scores were calculated using scripts created by the technical collaborators listed in the WAT2023 web page.[33] Note that AMFM scores were not produced for all tasks. For the Structured Document Translation task, we used only the XML-BLEU metric Hashimoto et al. (2019), which takes into account the accuracy of XML annotation transfer. All scores for each task were calculated using the corresponding reference translations.

Except for XML-BLEU, which uses this implementation for evaluation, the following preprocessing is done prior to computing scores. Before the calculation of the automatic evaluation scores, the translation results were tokenized or segmented with tokenization/segmentation tools for each language. For Japanese segmentation, we used three different tools: Juman version 7.0

[30] `https://github.com/tensorflow/tensor2tensor`

[31] `https://huggingface.co/facebook/mbart-large-50-many-to-many-mmt`

[32] `http://www.kecl.ntt.co.jp/icl/lirg/ribes/index.html`

[33] `lotus.kuee.kyoto-u.ac.jp/WAT/WAT2023/`

Figure 4: The interface for translation results submission

Kurohashi et al. (1994), KyTea 0.4.6 Neubig et al. (2011) with full SVM model[34] and MeCab 0.996 Kudo (2005) with IPA dictionary 2.7.0.[35] For Chinese segmentation, we used two different tools: KyTea 0.4.6 with full SVM Model in MSR model and Stanford Word Segmenter Tseng (2005) version 2014-06-16 with Chinese Penn Treebank (CTB) and Peking University (PKU)

[34] `http://www.phontron.com/kytea/model.html`

[35] `http://code.google.com/p/mecab/downloads/detail?name=mecab-ipadic-2.7.0-20070801.tar.gz`

model.[36] For Korean segmentation, we used mecab-ko.[37] For Myanmar and Khmer segmentations, we used `myseg.py`[38] and `kmseg.py`.[39] For English, French and Russian tokenizations, we used `tokenizer.perl`[40] in the Moses toolkit. For Indonesian, Malay, and Vietnamese tokenizations, we used `tokenizer.perl` actually sticking to the English tokenization settings. For Thai tokenization, we segmented the text at each individual character. For Assamese, Bengali, Gujarati, Hindi, Kannada, Malayalam, Marathi, Nepali, Odia, Punjabi, Sindhi, Sinhala, Tamil, Telugu, and Urdu tokenizations, we used Indic NLP Library[41] Kunchukuttan (2020). The detailed procedures for the automatic evaluation are shown on the WAT evaluation web page.[42]

5.2 Automatic Evaluation System

The automatic evaluation system receives translation results by participants and automatically gives evaluation scores to the uploaded results. As shown in Figure 4, the system requires participants to provide the following information for each submission:

- Human Evaluation: whether or not they submit the results for human evaluation;
- Publish the results of the evaluation: whether or not they permit to publish automatic evaluation scores on the WAT2023 web page;
- Task: the task you submit the results for;
- Used Other Resources: whether or not they used additional resources; and
- Method: the type of the method including SMT, RBMT, SMT and RBMT, EBMT, NMT and Other.

Evaluation scores of translation results that participants permit to be published are disclosed via the WAT2023 evaluation web page. Participants can also submit the results for human evaluation using the same web interface.

This automatic evaluation system will remain available even after WAT2023. Anybody can register an account for the system by the procedures described in the application site.[43]

5.3 A Note on AMFM Scores

Unlike previous years we do not compute AMFM scores on all tasks due to low participation this year. For readers interested in AMFM and recent advances, we refer readers to the following literature: Zhang et al. (2021b,a); D'Haro et al. (2019); Banchs et al. (2015b).

6 Human Evaluation

In WAT2023, we conducted *JPO adequacy evaluation* (Section 6.1).

[36] http://nlp.stanford.edu/software/segmenter.shtml
[37] https://bitbucket.org/eunjeon/mecab-ko/
[38] http://lotus.kuee.kyoto-u.ac.jp/WAT/my-en-data/wat2020.my-en.zip
[39] http://lotus.kuee.kyoto-u.ac.jp/WAT/km-en-data/km-en.zip
[40] https://github.com/moses-smt/mosesdecoder/tree/RELEASE-2.1.1/scripts/tokenizer/tokenizer.perl
[41] https://github.com/anoopkunchukuttan/indic_nlp_library
[42] http://lotus.kuee.kyoto-u.ac.jp/WAT/evaluation/index.html
[43] http://lotus.kuee.kyoto-u.ac.jp/WAT/WAT2023/application/index.html

5	All important information is transmitted correctly. (100%)
4	Almost all important information is transmitted correctly. (80%–)
3	More than half of important information is transmitted correctly. (50%–)
2	Some of important information is transmitted correctly. (20%–)
1	Almost all important information is NOT transmitted correctly. (–20%)

Table 9: The JPO adequacy criterion

6.1 JPO Adequacy Evaluation

We conducted JPO adequacy evaluation for the top two or three participants' systems of pairwise evaluation for each subtask.[44] The evaluation was carried out by translation experts based on the JPO adequacy evaluation criterion, which is originally defined by JPO to assess the quality of translated patent documents.

6.1.1 Sentence Selection and Evaluation

For the JPO adequacy evaluation, the 200 test sentences were randomly selected from the test sentences.

For each test sentence, input source sentence, translation by participants' system, and reference translation were shown to the annotators. To guarantee the quality of the evaluation, each sentence was evaluated by two annotators. Note that the selected sentences are basically the same as those used in the previous workshop.

6.1.2 Evaluation Criterion

Table 9 shows the JPO adequacy criterion from 5 to 1. The evaluation is performed subjectively. "Important information" represents the technical factors and their relationships. The degree of importance of each element is also considered in evaluating. The percentages in each grade are rough indications for the transmission degree of the source sentence meanings. For Structured Document Translation, we instructed the evaluators to consider the XML structure accuracy between the source, the translation and the reference. The detailed criterion is described in the JPO document (in Japanese).[45]

7 Evaluation Results

In this section, the evaluation results for WAT2023 are reported from several perspectives. Some of the results for both automatic and human evaluations are also accessible at the WAT2023 website.[46]

7.1 Official Evaluation Results

Figures 5, 6 and 7 show the evaluation results of Multimodal subtasks. Each figure contains the JPO adequacy evaluation result and evaluation summary of top systems. The detailed automatic evaluation results are shown in Appendix A.

[44] The number of systems varies depending on the subtasks.

[45] http://www.jpo.go.jp/shiryou/toushin/chousa/tokkyohonyaku_hyouka.htm

[46] http://lotus.kuee.kyoto-u.ac.jp/WAT/evaluation/

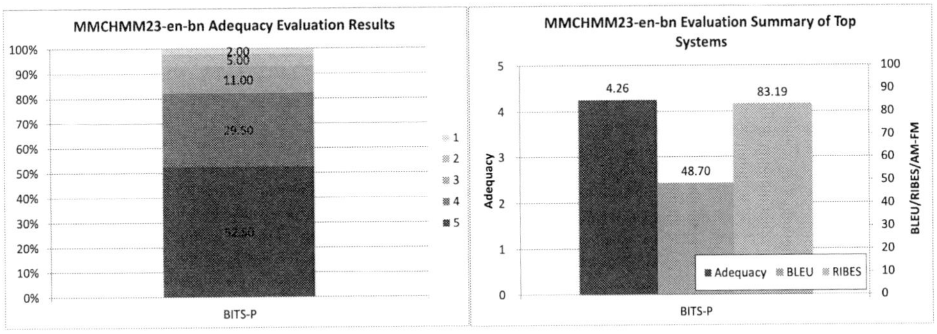

Figure 5: Official evaluation results of mmchmm23-en-bn.

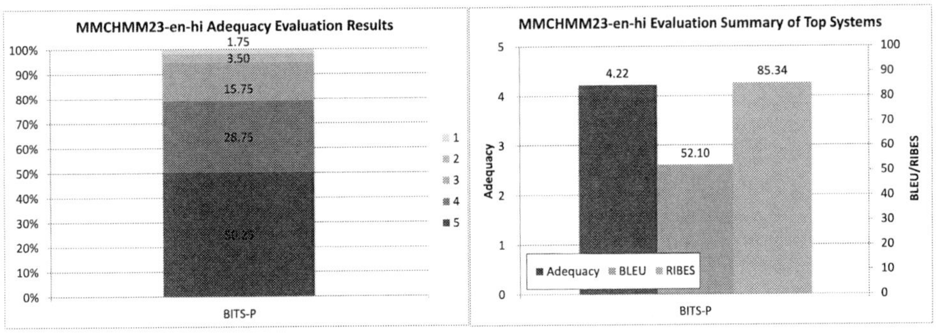

Figure 6: Official evaluation results of mmchmm23-en-hi.

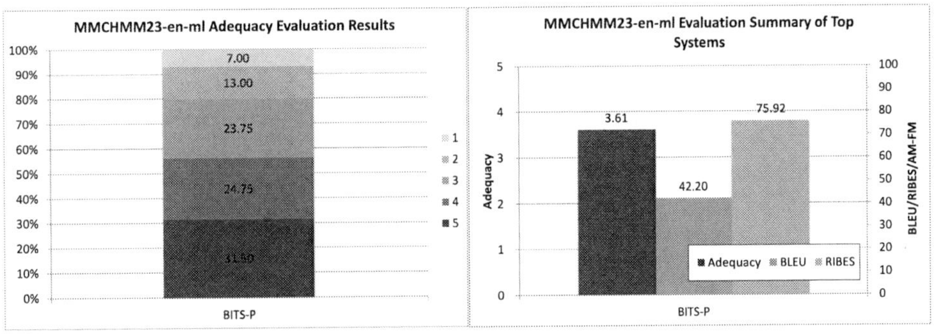

Figure 7: Official evaluation results of mmchmm23-en-ml.

8 Findings

8.1 English→Hindi Multi-Modal Task

This year two teams participated in the different sub-tasks (TEXT, MM) of the English→Hindi Multi-Modal task. The WAT2023 automatic evaluation scores for the participating teams are shown in Tables 11, 14, 17 and 20.

For the text-only sub-task (TEXT), one team "ODIAGEN" participated in the evaluation (E-Test) and challenge (C-Test) set by fine-tuning the *Transformer* model using NLLB-200 from Facebook. Their scores were outperformed in comparison to all previous years' submissions. It is worth mentioning, they did not use any additional resources.

For the multimodal sub-task (MM), we received two submissions from the teams "ODIAGEN", and "BITS-P", respectively. The team "BITS-P" obtained a BLEU score of *45.00* for the evaluation (E-Test) by NLLB model finetuning on captions with object tags of original and synthetic images using DETR model. The team "BITS-P" used additional resources for their model building. The team "ODIAGEN" obtained BLEU score of *41.60* by using image features (extracting object tags) appended with text and MBART finetuning. For the challenge (C-Test) set, both teams ("BITS-P", and "ODIAGEN") obtained BLEU scores of *52.10* and *42.80* respectively following the same approaches as in E-Test.

Human evaluation was done for the challenge test set multimodal translation (MM) as shown in Figure 6.

8.2 English→Malayalam Multi-Modal Task

This year two teams "ODIAGEN", and "BITS-P" participated in the different sub-tasks (TEXT, MM) of the English→ Malayalam Multi-Modal task. The WAT2023 automatic evaluation scores are shown in the Table 21, 15, 18, 12.

For the English to Malayalam text-only translation, team "ODIAGEN" obtained a BLEU score of *46.60*, and *39.70* for the evaluation (E-Test) and challenge (C-Test) respectively. They used fine-tuning Transformer using NLLB-200 from Facebook. For multimodal, the team "BITS-P" obtained a BLEU score of *51.90* for the evaluation test set and a BLEU score of *42.20* for the challenge test set. They used NLLB model finetuned on captions along with object tags of original and synthetic images using the DETR model.

Human evaluation was done for the challenge test set multimodal translation (MM) as shown in Figure 7.

8.3 English→Bengali Multi-Modal Task

This year two teams participated in the different sub-tasks (TEXT, MM) of the English→Bengali Multi-Modal task. The WAT2023 automatic evaluation scores are shown in the Table 22, 16, 19, 13.

For the text-only sub-task (TEXT), one team "ODIAGEN" participated in the evaluation (E-Test) and challenge (C-Test) set by fine-tuning the *Transformer* model using NLLB-200 from Facebook. Their scores were outperformed in comparison to all previous years' submissions.

For the multimodal sub-task (MM), we received two submissions from the teams "ODIAGEN", and "BITS-P", respectively. The team "BITS-P" obtained a BLEU score of *50.60* for the evaluation (E-Test) test set using the NLLB model finetuned on captions along with object tags of original and synthetic images using the DETR model. They used additional resources. The team "ODIAGEN" obtained a BLEU score of *43.90* by using transliteration-based phrase pairs augmentation and visual features in training using a BRNN encoder and doubly-attentive-rnn decoder. For the challenge (C-Test) test, for the same configuration, both teams obtained a BLEU score of *48.70* and 30.50 respectively.

Human evaluation was done for the challenge test set multimodal translation (MM) as

Model		Test (WAT 2023)			Test (WAT 2020)
		# Non-repetitive	# Repetitive	# Error	BLEU (%)
baseline	# Acceptable	**19 (11.0%)**	71 (41.0%)	0 (0.0%)	15.6
	# Unacceptable	29 (16.8%)	49 (28.3%)	5 (2.9%)	

Table 10: Evaluation results of the non-repetitive translation task. # Error indicates the number of translations where the target words/phrases themselves are mistranslated, undertranslated or overtranslated. As a reference, we also computed a BLEU score (Papineni et al., 2002b) on the test set II of the WAT2020 Newswire tasks (Nakazawa et al., 2020b) using SacreBLEU (Post, 2018).[47]

shown in Figure 5.

8.4 Non-Repetitive Translation Task

Although we did not receive any submissions in the non-repetitive translation task, we report the evaluation results of the baseline model in this new task. The results are presented in Table 10. The number of acceptable translations was about half of the test set. In addition, 79% $(71/(19+71))$ of the acceptable translations were written in a repetitive style. For the acceptable and non-repetitive outputs, the numbers of reductions and substitutions were 7 and 12, respectively. (For the unacceptable and non-repetitive outputs, the numbers of reductions and substitutions were 10 and 19, respectively.) This indicates that there is a lot of room for improvement in this task.

9 Conclusion and Future Perspective

This paper summarizes the shared tasks of WAT2023. This year, we had 2 participants who submitted their translation results. Both teams participated to the Indic multimodal translation tasks. This year we had smaller number of participants compared to the previous years. For the next WAT workshop, we want attract much more people to join our shared tasks.

Acknowledgement

The English→Hindi English→Malayalam, and English→Bengali Multi-Modal shared tasks were supported by the following grants at Silo AI and Charles University. The authors do not see any significant ethical or privacy concerns that would prevent the processing of the data used in the study. The datasets do not contain any personal data. Personal data of annotators needed when the datasets were prepared and when the outputs were evaluated were processed in compliance with the GDPR and national law.

- At Silo AI, the work was supported by SiloGen.
- At Charles University, the work was supported by the grant 19-26934X (NEUREM3) of the Czech Science Foundation and using language resources distributed by the LINDAT/CLARIN project of the Ministry of Education, Youth and Sports of the Czech Republic (projects LM2015071 and OP VVV VI CZ.02.1.01/0.0/0.0/16013/0001781).

The Restricted Translation is supported by Microsoft. The Non-Repetitive Translation task was supported by the commissioned research (No. 225) by National Institute of Information and Communications Technology (NICT), Japan.

[47]The signature is `nrefs:1|case:mixed|eff:no|tok:13a|smooth:exp|version:2.3.1`.

References

AI4Bharat, Gala, J., Chitale, P. A., AK, R., Doddapaneni, S., Gumma, V., Kumar, A., Nawale, J., Sujatha, A., Puduppully, R., Raghavan, V., Kumar, P., Khapra, M. M., Dabre, R., and Kunchukuttan, A. (2023). Indictrans2: Towards high-quality and accessible machine translation models for all 22 scheduled indian languages. *arXiv preprint arXiv: 2305.16307*.

Banchs, R. E., D'Haro, L. F., and Li, H. (2015a). Adequacy-fluency metrics: Evaluating mt in the continuous space model framework. *IEEE/ACM Trans. Audio, Speech and Lang. Proc.*, 23(3):472–482.

Banchs, R. E., D' Haro, L. F., and Li, H. (2015b). Adequacy-fluency metrics: Evaluating mt in the continuous space model framework. *IEEE/ACM Transactions on Audio, Speech, and Language Processing*, 23(3):472–482.

Block, M. (1994). *Broadcast Newswriting: The RTNDA Reference Guide*. Bonus Books.

Buschbeck, B. and Exel, M. (2020). A parallel evaluation data set of software documentation with document structure annotation.

Cappon, R. J. (2019). *The Associated Press Guide to News Writing*. Peterson's, fourth edition.

Dabre, R., Chu, C., and Kunchukuttan, A. (2020). A survey of multilingual neural machine translation. *ACM Comput. Surv.*, 53(5).

Dabre, R., Shrotriya, H., Kunchukuttan, A., Puduppully, R., Khapra, M., and Kumar, P. (2022). IndicBART: A pre-trained model for indic natural language generation. In *Findings of the Association for Computational Linguistics: ACL 2022*, pages 1849–1863, Dublin, Ireland. Association for Computational Linguistics.

D'Haro, L. F., Banchs, R. E., Hori, C., and Li, H. (2019). Automatic evaluation of end-to-end dialog systems with adequacy-fluency metrics. *Computer Speech and Language*, 55:200–215.

Ding, C., Hnin Thu Zar Aye, Win Pa Pa, Khin Thandar Nwet, Khin Mar Soe, Utiyama, M., and Sumita, E. (2019). Towards Burmese (Myanmar) morphological analysis: Syllable-based tokenization and part-of-speech tagging. *ACM Transactions on Asian and Low-Resource Language Information Processing (TALLIP)*, 19(1):5.

Ding, C., Utiyama, M., and Sumita, E. (2018). NOVA: A feasible and flexible annotation system for joint tokenization and part-of-speech tagging. *ACM Transactions on Asian and Low-Resource Language Information Processing (TALLIP)*, 18(2):17.

Doddapaneni, S., Aralikatte, R., Ramesh, G., Goyal, S., Khapra, M. M., Kunchukuttan, A., and Kumar, P. (2023). Towards leaving no Indic language behind: Building monolingual corpora, benchmark and models for Indic languages. In *Proceedings of the 61st Annual Meeting of the Association for Computational Linguistics (Volume 1: Long Papers)*, pages 12402–12426, Toronto, Canada. Association for Computational Linguistics.

Gu, W., Song, H., Chu, C., and Kurohashi, S. (2021). Video-guided machine translation with spatial hierarchical attention network. In *Proceedings of the 59th Annual Meeting of the Association for Computational Linguistics and the 11th International Joint Conference on Natural Language Processing: Student Research Workshop*, pages 87–92.

Hashimoto, K., Buschiazzo, R., Bradbury, J., Marshall, T., Socher, R., and Xiong, C. (2019). A high-quality multilingual dataset for structured documentation translation. In *Proceedings of the Fourth Conference on Machine Translation (Volume 1: Research Papers)*, pages 116–127, Florence, Italy. Association for Computational Linguistics.

Imankulova, A., Dabre, R., Fujita, A., and Imamura, K. (2019). Exploiting out-of-domain parallel data through multilingual transfer learning for low-resource neural machine translation. In *Proceedings of Machine Translation Summit XVII: Research Track*, pages 128–139, Dublin, Ireland. European Association for Machine Translation.

Isozaki, H., Hirao, T., Duh, K., Sudoh, K., and Tsukada, H. (2010). Automatic evaluation of translation quality for distant language pairs. In *Proceedings of the 2010 Conference on Empirical Methods in Natural Language Processing*, EMNLP '10, pages 944–952, Stroudsburg, PA, USA. Association for Computational Linguistics.

Johnson, M., Schuster, M., Le, Q. V., Krikun, M., Wu, Y., Chen, Z., Thorat, N., Viégas, F., Wattenberg, M., Corrado, G., Hughes, M., and Dean, J. (2017). Google's multilingual neural machine translation system: Enabling zero-shot translation. *Transactions of the Association for Computational Linguistics*, 5:339–351.

Khayrallah, H. and Koehn, P. (2018). On the impact of various types of noise on neural machine translation. In *Proceedings of the 2nd Workshop on Neural Machine Translation and Generation*, pages 74–83, Melbourne, Australia. Association for Computational Linguistics.

Klein, G., Kim, Y., Deng, Y., Senellart, J., and Rush, A. (2017). Opennmt: Open-source toolkit for neural machine translation. In *Proceedings of ACL 2017, System Demonstrations*, pages 67–72. Association for Computational Linguistics.

Kocmi, T., Bawden, R., Bojar, O., Dvorkovich, A., Federmann, C., Fishel, M., Gowda, T., Graham, Y., Grundkiewicz, R., Haddow, B., Knowles, R., Koehn, P., Monz, C., Morishita, M., Nagata, M., Nakazawa, T., Novák, M., Popel, M., and Popović, M. (2022). Findings of the 2022 conference on machine translation (WMT22). In *Proceedings of the Seventh Conference on Machine Translation (WMT)*, pages 1–45, Abu Dhabi, United Arab Emirates (Hybrid). Association for Computational Linguistics.

Koehn, P., Chaudhary, V., El-Kishky, A., Goyal, N., Chen, P.-J., and Guzmán, F. (2020). Findings of the WMT 2020 shared task on parallel corpus filtering and alignment. In *Proceedings of the Fifth Conference on Machine Translation*, pages 726–742, Online. Association for Computational Linguistics.

Kudo, T. (2005). Mecab : Yet another part-of-speech and morphological analyzer. *http://mecab.sourceforge.net/*.

Kunchukuttan, A. (2020). The IndicNLP Library. `https://github.com/anoopkunchukuttan/indic_nlp_library/blob/master/docs/indicnlp.pdf`.

Kurohashi, S., Nakamura, T., Matsumoto, Y., and Nagao, M. (1994). Improvements of Japanese morphological analyzer JUMAN. In *Proceedings of The International Workshop on Sharable Natural Language*, pages 22–28.

Lewis, M., Liu, Y., Goyal, N., Ghazvininejad, M., Mohamed, A., Levy, O., Stoyanov, V., and Zettlemoyer, L. (2020). BART: Denoising sequence-to-sequence pre-training for natural language generation, translation, and comprehension. In *Proceedings of the 58th Annual Meeting of the Association for Computational Linguistics*, pages 7871–7880, Online. Association for Computational Linguistics.

Li, Y., Shimizu, S., Gu, W., Chu, C., and Kurohashi, S. (2022). Visa: An ambiguous subtitles dataset for visual scene-aware machine translation. In *Proceedings of the 13th Language Resources and Evaluation Conference*, pages 6735–6743.

Liu, Y., Gu, J., Goyal, N., Li, X., Edunov, S., Ghazvininejad, M., Lewis, M., and Zettlemoyer, L. (2020). Multilingual denoising pre-training for neural machine translation. *Transactions of the Association for Computational Linguistics*, 8:726–742.

Merritt, A., Chu, C., and Arase, Y. (2020). A corpus for english-japanese multimodal neural machine translation with comparable sentences.

Morishita, M., Chousa, K., Suzuki, J., and Nagata, M. (2022). JParaCrawl v3.0: A large-scale English-Japanese parallel corpus. In *Proceedings of the Thirteenth Language Resources and Evaluation Conference*, pages 6704–6710, Marseille, France. European Language Resources Association.

Morishita, M., Suzuki, J., and Nagata, M. (2020). JParaCrawl: A large scale web-based English-Japanese parallel corpus. In *Proceedings of the 12th Language Resources and Evaluation Conference*, pages 3603–3609, Marseille, France. European Language Resources Association.

Nakazawa, T., Doi, N., Higashiyama, S., Ding, C., Dabre, R., Mino, H., Goto, I., Pa, W. P., Kunchukuttan, A., Oda, Y., Parida, S., Bojar, O., and Kurohashi, S. (2019). Overview of the 6th workshop on Asian translation. In *Proceedings of the 6th Workshop on Asian Translation*, pages 1–35, Hong Kong, China. Association for Computational Linguistics.

Nakazawa, T., Higashiyama, S., Ding, C., Mino, H., Goto, I., Kazawa, H., Oda, Y., Neubig, G., and Kurohashi, S. (2017). Overview of the 4th workshop on asian translation. In *Proceedings of the 4th Workshop on Asian Translation (WAT2017)*, pages 1–54. Asian Federation of Natural Language Processing.

Nakazawa, T., Mino, H., Goto, I., Dabre, R., Higashiyama, S., Parida, S., Kunchukuttan, A., Morishita, M., Bojar, O., Chu, C., Eriguchi, A., Abe, K., Oda, Y., and Kurohashi, S. (2022). Overview of the 9th workshop on Asian translation. In *Proceedings of the 9th Workshop on Asian Translation*, pages 1–36, Gyeongju, Republic of Korea. International Conference on Computational Linguistics.

Nakazawa, T., Nakayama, H., Ding, C., Dabre, R., Higashiyama, S., Mino, H., Goto, I., Pa, W. P., Kunchukuttan, A., Parida, S., et al. (2021a). Overview of the 8th workshop on asian translation. In *Proceedings of the 8th Workshop on Asian Translation (WAT2021)*, pages 1–45.

Nakazawa, T., Nakayama, H., Ding, C., Dabre, R., Higashiyama, S., Mino, H., Goto, I., Pa Pa, W., Kunchukuttan, A., Parida, S., Bojar, O., Chu, C., Eriguchi, A., Abe, K., Oda, Y., and Kurohashi, S. (2021b). Overview of the 8th workshop on Asian translation. In *Proceedings of the 8th Workshop on Asian Translation (WAT2021)*, pages 1–45, Online. Association for Computational Linguistics.

Nakazawa, T., Nakayama, H., Ding, C., Dabre, R., Higashiyama, S., Mino, H., Goto, I., Pa Pa, W., Kunchukuttan, A., Parida, S., Bojar, O., and Kurohashi, S. (2020a). Overview of the 7th workshop on Asian translation. In *Proceedings of the 7th Workshop on Asian Translation*, pages 1–44, Suzhou, China. Association for Computational Linguistics.

Nakazawa, T., Nakayama, H., Ding, C., Dabre, R., Kunchukuttan, A., Pa, W. P., Bojar, O., Parida, S., Goto, I., Mino, H., Manabe, H., Sudoh, K., Kurohashi, S., and Bhattacharyya, P., editors (2020b). *Proceedings of the 7th Workshop on Asian Translation*, Suzhou, China. Association for Computational Linguistics.

Nakazawa, T., Nakayama, H., Goto, I., Mino, H., Ding, C., Dabre, R., Kunchukuttan, A., Higashiyama, S., Manabe, H., Pa, W. P., Parida, S., Bojar, O., Chu, C., Eriguchi, A., Abe, K., Oda, Y., Sudoh, K., Kurohashi, S., and Bhattacharyya, P., editors (2021c). *Proceedings of the 8th Workshop on Asian Translation (WAT2021)*, Online. Association for Computational Linguistics.

Nakazawa, T., Sudoh, K., Higashiyama, S., Ding, C., Dabre, R., Mino, H., Goto, I., Pa, W. P., Kunchukuttan, A., and Kurohashi, S. (2018). Overview of the 5th workshop on Asian translation. In *Proceedings of the 32nd Pacific Asia Conference on Language, Information and Computation: 5th Workshop on Asian Translation: 5th Workshop on Asian Translation*, Hong Kong. Association for Computational Linguistics.

Neubig, G., Nakata, Y., and Mori, S. (2011). Pointwise prediction for robust, adaptable japanese morphological analysis. In *Proceedings of the 49th Annual Meeting of the Association for Computational Linguistics: Human Language Technologies: Short Papers - Volume 2*, HLT '11, pages 529–533, Stroudsburg, PA, USA. Association for Computational Linguistics.

Papineni, K., Roukos, S., Ward, T., and Zhu, W.-J. (2002a). Bleu: a method for automatic evaluation of machine translation. In *ACL*, pages 311–318.

Papineni, K., Roukos, S., Ward, T., and Zhu, W.-J. (2002b). Bleu: a method for automatic evaluation of machine translation. In *Proceedings of the 40th Annual Meeting of the Association for Computational Linguistics*, pages 311–318, Philadelphia, Pennsylvania, USA. Association for Computational Linguistics.

Papper, R. A. (2021). *Broadcast News and Writing Stylebook*. Routledge, seventh edition.

Parida, S. and Bojar, O. (2021). Malayalam visual genome 1.0. LINDAT/CLARIAH-CZ digital library at the Institute of Formal and Applied Linguistics (ÚFAL), Faculty of Mathematics and Physics, Charles University.

Parida, S., Bojar, O., and Dash, S. R. (2019a). Hindi visual genome: A dataset for multimodal english-to-hindi machine translation. *arXiv preprint arXiv:1907.08948*.

Parida, S., Bojar, O., and Dash, S. R. (2019b). Hindi Visual Genome: A Dataset for Multimodal English-to-Hindi Machine Translation. *Computación y Sistemas*. In print. Presented at CICLing 2019, La Rochelle, France.

Post, M. (2018). A call for clarity in reporting BLEU scores. In *Proceedings of the Third Conference on Machine Translation: Research Papers*, pages 186–191, Brussels, Belgium. Association for Computational Linguistics.

Ramesh, G., Doddapaneni, S., Bheemaraj, A., Jobanputra, M., AK, R., Sharma, A., Sahoo, S., Diddee, H., J, M., Kakwani, D., Kumar, N., Pradeep, A., Nagaraj, S., Deepak, K., Raghavan, V., Kunchukuttan, A., Kumar, P., and Khapra, M. S. (2022). Samanantar: The largest publicly available parallel corpora collection for 11 indic languages. *Transactions of the Association for Computational Linguistics*, 10:145–162.

Riza, H., Purwoadi, M., Uliniansyah, T., Ti, A. A., Aljunied, S. M., Mai, L. C., Thang, V. T., Thai, N. P., Chea, V., Sam, S., Seng, S., Khin Mar Soe, Khin Thandar Nwet, Utiyama, M., and Ding, C. (2016). Introduction of the asian language treebank. In *In Proc. of O-COCOSDA*, pages 1–6.

Sen, A., Parida, S., Kotwal, K., Panda, S., Bojar, O., and Dash, S. R. (2022). Bengali visual genome 1.0. LINDAT/CLARIAH-CZ digital library at the Institute of Formal and Applied Linguistics (ÚFAL), Faculty of Mathematics and Physics, Charles University.

Soky, K., Mimura, M., Kawahara, T., Li, S., Ding, C., Chu, C., and Sam, S. (2021). Khmer speech translation corpus of the extraordinary chambers in the courts of cambodia (eccc). In *2021 24th Conference of the Oriental COCOSDA International Committee for the Co-ordination and Standardisation of Speech Databases and Assessment Techniques (O-COCOSDA)*, pages 122–127.

Thu, Y. K., Pa, W. P., Utiyama, M., Finch, A., and Sumita, E. (2016). Introducing the Asian language treebank (ALT). In *Proceedings of the Tenth International Conference on Language Resources and Evaluation (LREC'16)*, pages 1574–1578, Portorož, Slovenia. European Language Resources Association (ELRA).

Tseng, H. (2005). A conditional random field word segmenter. In *In Fourth SIGHAN Workshop on Chinese Language Processing*.

Vaswani, A., Bengio, S., Brevdo, E., Chollet, F., Gomez, A., Gouws, S., Jones, L., Kaiser, Ł., Kalchbrenner, N., Parmar, N., Sepassi, R., Shazeer, N., and Uszkoreit, J. (2018). Tensor2tensor for neural machine translation. In *Proceedings of the 13th Conference of the Association for Machine Translation in the Americas (Volume 1: Research Papers)*, pages 193–199. Association for Machine Translation in the Americas.

Vaswani, A., Shazeer, N., Parmar, N., Uszkoreit, J., Jones, L., Gomez, A. N., Kaiser, L., and Polosukhin, I. (2017). Attention is all you need. *CoRR*, abs/1706.03762.

Yi Mon Shwe Sin and Khin Mar Soe (2018). Syllable-based myanmar-english neural machine translation. In *In Proc. of ICCA*, pages 228–233.

Zhang, C., D'Haro, L. F., Banchs, R. E., Friedrichs, T., and Li, H. (2021a). *Deep AM-FM: Toolkit for Automatic Dialogue Evaluation*, pages 53–69. Springer Singapore, Singapore.

Zhang, C., Lee, G., D'Haro, L. F., and Li, H. (2021b). D-score: Holistic dialogue evaluation without reference. *IEEE/ACM Transactions on Audio, Speech, and Language Processing*, pages 1–1.

Zhao, Y., Komachi, M., Kajiwara, T., and Chu, C. (2020). Double attention-based multimodal neural machine translation with semantic image regions. In *EAMT*, pages 105–114.

Appendix A Submissions

Tables 11 to 22 summarize translation results submitted to WAT2023. Type and RSRC columns indicate type of method and use of other resources.

System	ID	Type	RSRC	BLEU	RIBES	AMFM
BITS-P	7124	NMT	YES	52.10	0.853388	–
ODIAGEN	7106	NMT	NO	42.80	0.815156	–

Table 11: MMCHMM23 en-hi submissions

System	ID	Type	RSRC	BLEU	RIBES	AMFM
BITS-P	7126	NMT	YES	42.20	0.759248	–

Table 12: MMCHMM23 en-ml submissions

System	ID	Type	RSRC	BLEU	RIBES	AMFM
BITS-P	7122	NMT	YES	48.70	0.831946	–
ODIAGEN	7108	NMT	NO	30.50	0.690706	–

Table 13: MMCHMM23 en-bn submissions

System	ID	Type	RSRC	BLEU	RIBES	AMFM
ODIAGEN	7088	NMT	NO	53.60	0.858033	–
ODIAGEN	7110	NMT	NO	53.10	0.854334	–

Table 14: MMCHTEXT23 en-hi submissions

System	ID	Type	RSRC	BLEU	RIBES	AMFM
ODIAGEN	7112	NMT	NO	39.70	0.752401	–

Table 15: MMCHTEXT23 en-ml submissions

System	ID	Type	RSRC	BLEU	RIBES	AMFM
ODIAGEN	7090	NMT	NO	47.80	0.821982	–

Table 16: MMCHTEXT23 en-bn submissions

System	ID	Type	RSRC	BLEU	RIBES	AMFM
BITS-P	7125	NMT	YES	45.00	0.829320	–
ODIAGEN	7105	NMT	NO	41.60	0.811420	–

Table 17: MMEVMM23 en-hi submissions

System	ID	Type	RSRC	BLEU	RIBES	AMFM
BITS-P	7127	NMT	YES	51.90	0.799683	–

Table 18: MMEVMM23 en-ml submissions

System	ID	Type	RSRC	BLEU	RIBES	AMFM
BITS-P	7123	NMT	YES	50.60	0.814207	–
ODIAGEN	7107	NMT	NO	42.40	0.763497	–

Table 19: MMEVMM23 en-bn submissions

System	ID	Type	RSRC	BLEU	RIBES	AMFM
ODIAGEN	7087	NMT	NO	44.60	0.829217	–
ODIAGEN	7109	NMT	NO	44.60	0.829213	–

Table 20: MMEVTEXT23 en-hi submissions

System	ID	Type	RSRC	BLEU	RIBES	AMFM
ODIAGEN	7091	NMT	NO	46.60	0.746474	–
ODIAGEN	7111	NMT	NO	46.20	0.737472	–

Table 21: MMEVTEXT23 en-ml submissions

System	ID	Type	RSRC	BLEU	RIBES	AMFM
ODIAGEN	7089	NMT	NO	49.20	0.797703	–

Table 22: MMEVTEXT23 en-bn submissions

Mitigating Domain Mismatch in Machine Translation via Paraphrasing

Hyuga Koretaka[1] koretaka@ai.cs.ehime-u.ac.jp
Tomoyuki Kajiwara[1] kajiwara@cs.ehime-u.ac.jp
Atsushi Fujita[2] atsushi.fujita@nict.go.jp
Takashi Ninomiya[1] ninomiya@cs.ehime-u.ac.jp
[1]Graduate School of Science and Engineering, Ehime University, Ehime, Japan
[2]National Institute of Information and Communications Technology, Kyoto, Japan

Abstract

Quality of machine translation (MT) deteriorates significantly when translating texts having characteristics that differ from the training data, such as content domain. Although previous studies have focused on adapting MT models on a bilingual parallel corpus in the target domain, this approach is not applicable when no parallel data are available for the target domain or when utilizing black-box MT systems. To mitigate problems caused by such domain mismatch without relying on any corpus in the target domain, this study proposes a method to search for better translations by paraphrasing input texts of MT. To obtain better translations even for input texts from unforeknown domains, we generate their multiple paraphrases, translate each, and rerank the resulting translations to select the most likely one. Experimental results on Japanese-to-English translation reveal that the proposed method improves translation quality in terms of BLEU score for input texts from specific domains.

1 Introduction

Despite recent advances in machine translation (MT), translation quality still depends on the characteristics of the data on which the MT system is trained. Therefore, for input texts having significantly different characteristics from the training data, there is a risk that translation quality may be degraded (Koehn and Knowles, 2017). To alleviate mismatches in one of such characteristics, content domain (henceforth, domain), an approach of transfer learning (Chu and Wang, 2018) is commonly used, where a pre-trained MT model is fine-tuned on a parallel corpus in the target domain. However, there are many challenges in supporting a variety of domains. First of all, there are only a limited number of domains that have access to a bilingual parallel corpus sufficient for fine-tuning pre-trained MT models. Even if parallel corpora are available for a large number of domains, then the time required for fine-tuning for each domain and the management cost for resulting models will not be negligible. More importantly, existing domain adaptation methods are not applicable in situations where we target a black-box MT system, such as Google Translate and DeepL, even if they are already superior to pre-trained MT models in the domain of interest.

This paper proposes a method to bridge the domain gap between sentences to be translated and MT training data without a need for additional training for a specific target domain as in existing domain adaptation methods, such as fine-tuning pre-trained MT models on human-made

Proceedings of the 10th Workshop on Asian Translation, pages 29–40
September 4, 2023, Macau SAR, China

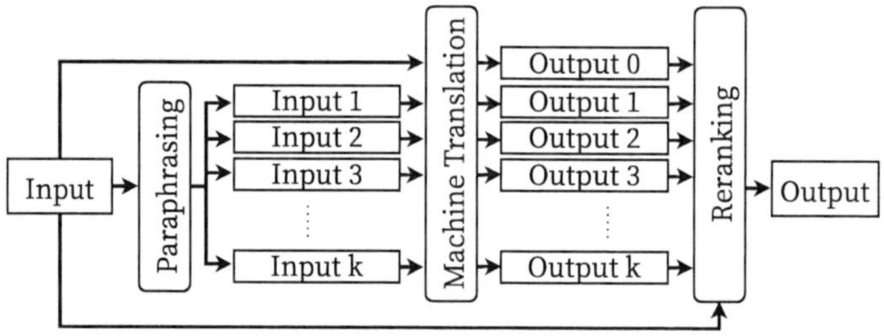

Figure 1: Overview of the proposed method.

and/or synthetic in-domain parallel data. As shown in Figure 1, our method first generates multiple paraphrases from a given input sentence, generates translation candidates using the given black-box MT system (henceforth, target MT system), and finally reranks those candidates to select the best one. We assume that diverse paraphrases of the sentences to be translated could include expressions that are less deviated for the target MT system, and such paraphrase could lead to an improvement of translation quality. The proposed method has the advantage that it requires neither fine-tuning the MT model nor any bilingual parallel corpus in the target domain. Our controlled experiment on Japanese-to-English translation revealed that the proposed method improves translation quality in terms of BLEU score in the domains that are not covered when training the target MT system.

2 Related Work

Paraphrasing input sentences has improved the performance of various natural language processing tasks such as document summarization (Siddharthan et al., 2004) and information extraction (Evans, 2011). Paraphrasing has been studied also for MT. Miyata and Fujita (2017, 2021) investigated manual pre-editing, including paraphrasing, to push the limit of existing MT services, and identified diverse types of pre-editing that can improve translation quality. However, there are two issues in automating paraphrasing for MT. One is that we lack a method for producing diverse (and accurate) paraphrases. Past work on automatic paraphrasing for MT (Štajner and Popović, 2016, 2018; Mehta et al., 2020) has examined only a limited variation, i.e., lexical and/or syntactic simplification, and observed quality improvement only in limited settings. Another issue is that the effect of each particular paraphrasing is unpredictable due to the sensitivity of neural MT to input sentences (Miyata and Fujita, 2021). We thus need to assess the quality of MT outputs in a post-hoc manner rather than the quality of paraphrased sentences before translating them with the target MT system.

3 Proposed Method

To automatically bridge the gap between the domains of input sentences and MT training data, we propose a framework consisting of three steps shown in Figure 1. Given an input sentence, we generate multiple paraphrases for it, translate each of the input sentence and multiple paraphrases using the target MT system, and select one candidate translation through reranking.

In this section, we describe the first paraphrasing step and the third reranking step. For the second step, i.e., MT, we primarily assume a black-box system, such as online MT services. However, to explore better reranking, we also consider a glass-box setting, assuming that some information can be drawn from the target MT system.

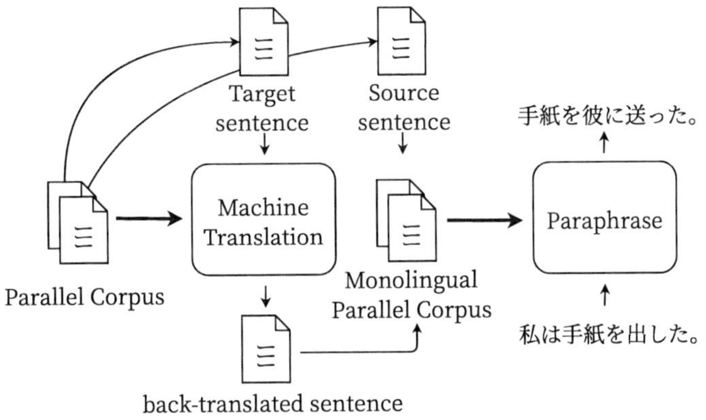

Figure 2: Sentence-level paraphrase.

3.1 Paraphrasing

Given a sentence to be translated, we can assume that there must be a paraphrase of it which can be better translated by the target MT system. However, it is difficult to know in advance which paraphrases are more likely to be better translated by the target MT system (Miyata and Fujita, 2021). Instead of determining the best paraphrase of the input sentence for the MT system, we leave the selection for the post MT step.

We consider generating multiple paraphrases both at sentence and word levels. Whereas sentence-level paraphrasing aims to paraphrase entire sentences using a sequence-to-sequence model, word-level paraphrasing focuses on altering single words relying on a masked language model and word embeddings.

Sentence-level Paraphrasing: Following previous work, we regard sentence-level paraphrasing as a sequence-to-sequence task. There are two conceivable options: back-translation-based approach (Wieting and Gimpel, 2018) illustrated in Figure 2 and monolingual translation-based approach (Thompson and Post, 2020b). The back-translation-based approach relies on a bilingual parallel corpus of the source language and an arbitrary target language. First, we train a translation model from the target language to the source language on the parallel corpus. Through translating the target side of the parallel corpus into the source language and coupling them with the source sentences in the parallel corpus, we automatically obtain a monolingual parallel corpus in the source language. Using this monolingual parallel corpus, we train a paraphrasing model[1], placing the back-translated sentences at the source side. On the other hand, the monolingual translation-based approach uses a pre-trained multilingual MT model that covers the source language. The model has been trained only on the bilingual parallel data, but no parallel data on the same language for paraphrasing; nevertheless, it is inherently capable of generating paraphrases provided that the language appears both in the source and target side during pre-training. We generate sentence-level paraphrases by specifying the same language for both source and target. For both approaches, given an input sentence, we generate its k paraphrases with the paraphrase models by performing a beam search with a beam size of k.

Word-level Paraphrasing: For word-level paraphrasing, we propose a method based on a pre-trained masked language model and pre-trained word embeddings both covering the source

[1]We refer to the back-translation-based paraphrase model as Denoiser.

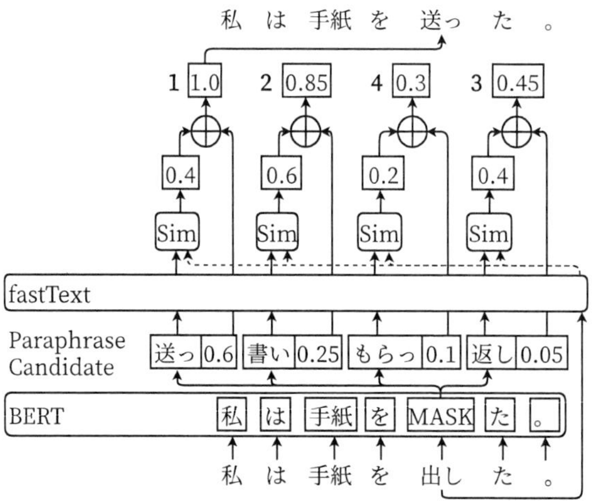

Figure 3: Word-level paraphrase.

language. As illustrated in Figure 3, our method consists of two steps: candidate generation and (word-level) reranking. Let $X = x_1, \ldots, x_{|X|}$ be an input sentence consisting of $|X|$ words. First, we generate the top n paraphrase candidates for each word x_i ($1 \leq i \leq |X|$): the input sentence with each word x_i masked is input to the masked language model and n-best words[2] according to their probability are output. Then, among ($|X| \times n$) paraphrase candidates, we select top k candidates. For this reranking, we use the sum of the probability of the masked language model and the cosine similarity of static word embeddings of the original word x_i and the paraphrase candidate.

3.2 Reranking

As shown in Figure 1, the reranking step selects one translation among $(k + 1)$ candidates generated by the target MT system for each of the input sentence and its k paraphrases. Various features have been proposed for reranking translation candidates (Marie and Fujita, 2018; Kiyono et al., 2020), but most of them are not available when we target a black-box MT system, such as Google Translate and DeepL. Therefore, we implement a reranking method for such an MT system relying only on a simple translation likelihood score that can be drawn from freely available MT models, such as mBART (Tang et al., 2020) and M2M-100 (Fan et al., 2021). We call this black-box reranking, since no information is retrieved from the target MT system. On the other hand, if the target MT system can give a score for a given pair of source sentence and translation candidate, such score should better help reranking. We therefore also examine this glass-box reranking.

Black-box Reranking: In black-box reranking, we use a multilingual MT model that covers both the source and target languages. As in previous work (Thompson and Post, 2020a; Kiyono et al., 2020), we compute the forced-decoding score[3] from the input sentence to each translation candidate. Additionally, forced-decoding score from each candidate to the input sentence is computed and the candidates are reranked simply by the average of the forced decoding scores for the two directions.

[2]This may include x_i itself.

[3]e.g., log probability normalized by the length.

Glass-box Reranking: In glass-box reranking, we use the target MT model and another MT model for the backward translation direction, i.e., the target language to the source language. Given a pair of the input sentence and the translation candidate, we compute forced-decoding scores for both translation directions using these models in the same manner with the black-box reranking, and the candidates are simply reranked by the average of these scores. Note that the score from the input sentence to each candidate should have already been given during the previous MT decoding step.

4 Experiments

We evaluated the effectiveness of the proposed method on three Japanese-to-English translation tasks. For the sake of fair comparison, in our work, we built an MT system by ourselves instead of using a truly black-box one.

4.1 Settings

Data: To train the target MT system, we randomly extracted 10 million sentence pairs for training and another 2,000 sentence pairs for validation from JParaCrawl[4] (Morishita et al., 2022). To train a sentence-level paraphrasing model with the back-translation-based approach, we randomly extracted 10 million sentence pairs for training and another 2,000 sentence pairs for validation from the remaining part of JParaCrawl.

We used three test sets on specific domains. One is ASPEC (Nakazawa et al., 2016), an excerpt from scientific papers, consisting of 1,812 sentence pairs. Second one is the test set used in WMT20 Shared Task on News (Barrault et al., 2020), an excerpt from news domain consisting of 993 sentence pairs. Last one is MTNT2019, the test set used in WMT 2019 Machine Translation Robustness Shared Task (Li et al., 2019) excerpted from the Reddit discussion website, consisting of 1,100 sentence pairs.[5] For reference, we randomly extracted 2,000 sentence pairs from JParaCrawl as an general-domain[6] test set. Note that they do not overlap with the training and validation sets used for the MT and sentence-level paraphrasing models.

As a preprocessing step, we first removed duplicates and split the data from JParaCrawl. We then applied NFKC normalization to all train/validation data and the source side of test data,[7] and then trained unigram-based subwording models (Kudo, 2018) on the training data using SentencePiece[8] (Kudo and Richardson, 2018). For MT, we obtained two separate vocabularies of 32,000 subwords for Japanese and English, respectively, and then applied the model to the training and validation data in their respective language. For sentence-level paraphrasing model with the back-translation-based approach, we first generated a monolingual parallel corpus by back-translating the English side of the sampled parallel data into Japanese, and then trained a single model covering 32,000 subwords on the training part of the monolingual parallel corpus. Both sides of the training and validation data were tokenized with the obtained SentencePiece model. We set the character coverage option of sentencepiece to 1.0 and 0.9998 for English and Japanese, respectively.

When inputting the source side of the test data to our sentence-level paraphrasing model, it was tokenized using the corresponding model. Sentence-level paraphrases were once detokenized with the same model, and again tokenized using the model trained on the Japanese side of the sampled bilingual parallel data before the succeeding MT step.

[4] `https://www.kecl.ntt.co.jp/icl/lirg/jparacrawl/`, v3.0

[5] `https://pmichel31415.github.io/mtnt/`, with an empty line 1,033 excluded.

[6] JParaCrawl can be considered as a general-domain parallel corpus, because it covers various domains seen on the Internet.

[7] We left the target side of the test data unprocessed, i.e., reference translations, following Post (2018).

[8] `https://github.com/google/sentencepiece/`

Models: We trained a Transformer Base model (Vaswani et al., 2017) for MT, sentence-level paraphrasing, and the backward MT for glass-box reranking with Fairseq[9] (Ott et al., 2019). We trained these models using mini-batch size of $60,000$ tokens, a learning rate of 5×10^{-4}, dropout of 0.1, label smoothing of 0.1, and Adam optimizer with $\beta_1 = 0.9$ and $\beta_2 = 0.98$. We computed the cross-entropy loss for the validation data every 1,500 steps and stopped the training after 10 consecutive times without an improvement of the best cross-entropy loss. We ran the model training only once on three A6000 GPUs, which consumed 22 and 26 hours for the MT and sentence-level paraphrasing models, respectively. For inference of MT in our framework, we used 1-best output generated by beam search with a beam size of 5 and the length penalty of 1.0.

To implement sentence-level paraphrasing with the back-translation-based approach, we generated back-translated sentences using a multilingual MT model called M2M-100[10] (Fan et al., 2021). On the other hand, to implement the monolingual translation-based approach, we used M2M-100 and mBART fine-tuned for multilingual translation[11] (Tang et al., 2020) separately for the sake of comparison. Note that none of these models have been fine-tuned on any paraphrase-specific data.

To implement the word-level paraphrasing model, we exclusively used Japanese model of BERT (Devlin et al., 2019) (JaBERT[12]) and multilingual model of BERT (mBERT[13]) as the masked language model, and the Japanese model of fastText[14] (Bojanowski et al., 2017) as the word embeddings. We set the number of candidate paraphrases n for each word to 10.

To implement black-box reranking, we used mBART.[9]

Comparison Method: As a comparison method without paraphrasing, we output one translation for each input sentence using beam search with a beam size of $(k + 1)$. Also, we output $(k + 1)$ candidate translations for each input sentence using beam search with a beam size of $(k + 1)$, assuming such a functionality in the given black-box MT system, and reranked them in the same manner as the third step in our framework.

Evaluation Metric: To evaluate the quality of translation, we computed BLEU score (Papineni et al., 2002) using SacreBLEU[15] (Post, 2018). To determine if differences in BLEU scores are significant, we performed statistical significance testing ($p < 0.05$) based on paired bootstrap resampling implemented in SacreBLEU.

4.2 Results of Individual Paraphrasing Methods

Table 1 shows the BLEU scores of our methods and baseline methods that do not use any paraphrasing method, where the oracle results based on the best sentence-level BLEU scores are also presented.

First, we focus on the paraphrase generation method. In ASPEC and WMT20, word-level paraphrasing (Models (3)–(4) and (9)–(10) in Table 1) consistently performed better than sentence-level paraphrasing (Models (5)–(7) and (11)–(13)). In contrast, in MTNT2019 and JParaCrawl, the word-level and sentence-level paraphrasing methods were not superior or inferior to each other. Overall, the oracle results show that word-level paraphrasing (Models (15)–

[9] `https://github.com/facebookresearch/fairseq/`
[10] `https://huggingface.co/facebook/m2m100_418M/`
[11] `https://huggingface.co/facebook/mbart-large-50-many-to-many-mmt/`
[12] `https://huggingface.co/cl-tohoku/bert-base-japanese-whole-word-masking/`
[13] `https://huggingface.co/bert-base-multilingual-cased/`
[14] `https://fasttext.cc/docs/en/crawl-vectors.html`
[15] `https://github.com/mjpost/sacrebleu/`
Short signature: `BLEU|#:1|c:mixed|e:no|tok:13a|s:exp|v:2.3.1`

(16)) has a larger potential compared to sentence-level paraphrasing (Models (17)–(19)), and in fact word-level paraphrasing methods have performed more effectively than sentence-level paraphrasing.

Next, we focus on the domain of evaluation data. In ASPEC and WMT20, word-level paraphrasing (Models (3)–(4) and (9)–(10)) consistently showed the best performance. On the other hand, in MTNT2019 and JParaCrawl, paraphrasing caused either no change or a degradation in translation quality. As for MTNT2019, the oracle BLEU scores (Models (14)–(19)) show that the gains are comparably large with those for ASPEC and WMT20 tasks. We therefore consider that the poor results for MTNT2019 are attributed to the versatility of the pre-trained MT models used for reranking, i.e., mBART and our own models based on JParaCrawl; they have not been trained on translations of less formal texts, such as user-generated contents in MTNT2019, and thus were not capable of selecting appropriate translations among candidates. In contrast, the oracle BLEU scores for JParaCrawl are substantially lower than those based on beam search, indicating the poor potential of our paraphrasing methods. One possible explanation for this is that there is no domain gap between the input sentences and the MT model, and paraphrasing may make the sentences unsuitable for the MT model.

Finally, we focus on the number of paraphrases, i.e., k. In ASPEC and WMT20, translation quality improved as k increased in the black-box reranking of word-level paraphrases (Models (3)–(4)) and glass-box reranking (Models (9)–(13)). In contrast, in MTNT2019 and JParaCrawl, translation quality decreased or remained the same even when k was increased.

4.3 Results of Combinations of Paraphrasing Methods

Having evaluated the sentence-level and word-level paraphrasing methods, we explored whether their combinations further boost the translation quality. Combination here means the merger of two sets of $(k+1)$ translation candidates, which results in $(2k+1)$ candidates since two sets contain an identical one, i.e., the translation for the original input sentence.

Table 2 shows the BLEU scores of all the combinations of word-level and sentence-level paraphrasing methods and the baseline methods that do not use any paraphrasing method but rely on $(2k+1)$ translation candidates obtained by beam search. Compared to the results for the word-level methods only (Models (3)–(4) and (9)–(10) in Table 1), most of the combinations resulted in either no change or degeneration on BLEU scores. Even though some conditions in WMT20 and MTNT2019 tasks have some benefits from the combination, we recommend to use the word-level paraphrasing methods alone rather than combining them with sentence-level paraphrasing methods.

4.4 Analysis of Translations for Paraphrases

Figure 4 shows the percentage of candidate translations for paraphrases that have an increased sentence-level BLEU score compared to the translation for the original sentence. For all paraphrase generation methods, about 20–30% of candidate translations for paraphrases improved the BLEU score compared to the translations for the original sentences. For word-level paraphrasing, which was the most effective paraphrase generation method, the percentages increased as k increased. Therefore, we consider that increasing k is effective in obtaining better candidate translations, even though it increases the cost for generating candidates.

	Paraphrasing		Reranking	ASPEC			WMT20			MTNT2019			JParaCrawl		
ID	Level	Model	Model	$k=5$	$k=10$	$k=20$	$k=5$	$k=10$	$k=20$	$k=5$	$k=10$	$k=20$	$k=5$	$k=10$	$k=20$
(1)	-	-	-	20.5	20.7	20.6	20.6	20.9	20.8	15.5	15.6	15.9	34.6	34.6	34.5
(2)	-	-	mBART (black-box)	20.6	20.8	21.1*	20.8	21.2*	21.4*	**15.8**	**15.9**	**15.9**	**34.1***	**33.9***	**33.4***
(3)	Word	JaBERT		20.9*	21.0	20.8	**21.5***	**21.8***	**21.9***	15.6	15.6	15.5	33.3*	32.9*	32.6*
(4)	Word	mBERT		**21.1***	**21.2***	**21.2***	21.2*	21.4*	21.8*	15.4	15.3	15.4	33.3*	33.1*	32.7*
(5)	Sentence	mBART		20.3	20.1*	20.1*	20.3	20.4*	20.4*	14.8*	14.6*	14.7*	33.1*	32.9*	32.2*
(6)	Sentence	M2M-100		19.9*	19.8*	19.7*	20.8	20.6	20.8	15.3	15.2	14.5*	32.9*	32.5*	32.0*
(7)	Sentence	Denoiser		20.4	20.3*	20.4	20.7	20.9	20.9	15.5	15.3	15.4	33.8*	33.1*	32.9*
(8)	-	-	MT (glass-box)	20.7	21.1*	21.2*	20.8	20.9	21.2*	15.8*	**15.9**	**15.9**	**34.7**	**34.7**	34.3
(9)	Word	JaBERT		**21.2***	**21.4***	21.2*	**21.6***	**22.0***	21.9*	**15.9***	15.7	15.5	34.5	34.5	34.3
(10)	Word	mBERT		**21.2***	21.3*	**21.6***	**21.6***	21.8*	**22.1***	15.7	15.4	15.5	34.5	34.4	34.0*
(11)	Sentence	mBART		20.8*	20.7	21.0*	21.0*	20.9	21.1	15.4	15.5	15.4	**34.7**	34.6	34.6
(12)	Sentence	M2M-100		20.6	20.6	20.6	21.2*	21.4*	21.5*	15.8	**15.9**	15.7	34.6	**34.7**	**34.7**
(13)	Sentence	Denoiser		20.6	20.7	20.8	20.9*	20.9	21.2*	15.8	15.7	15.8	**34.7**	**34.7**	**34.7**
(14)	-	-	Oracle	**24.3**	26.0	**27.9**	23.6	25.3	26.8	19.0	20.2	**22.0**	**38.6**	**40.1**	**41.5**
(15)	Word	JaBERT		**24.3**	25.9	27.4	24.9	**26.3**	27.6	**19.3**	**20.4**	21.8	37.8	38.7	39.8
(16)	Word	mBERT		**24.3**	**26.1**	**27.9**	**25.0**	26.2	**27.7**	19.0	**20.4**	21.7	37.6	38.6	39.7
(17)	Sentence	mBART		23.4	24.4	25.4	23.1	23.8	24.8	17.8	18.3	19.2	36.4	37.1	37.6
(18)	Sentence	M2M-100		23.6	24.5	25.5	23.8	24.5	25.5	18.2	19.0	19.8	36.6	37.1	37.7
(19)	Sentence	Denoiser		23.5	24.6	25.8	23.7	24.7	25.4	18.4	19.3	20.3	36.7	37.4	38.1

Table 1: BLEU scores (k: number of paraphrases, **bold**: the highest BLEU score of each reranking result by column, *: statistically significant difference ($p < 0.05$) over the baseline method in the first row.)

	Paraphrasing		Reranking	ASPEC			WMT20			MTNT2019			JParaCrawl		
ID	Level	Model	Model	$k = 5$	$k = 10$	$k = 20$	$k = 5$	$k = 10$	$k = 20$	$k = 5$	$k = 10$	$k = 20$	$k = 5$	$k = 10$	$k = 20$
(1)	-	-	-	20.7	20.6	20.8	20.9	20.8	20.7	15.6	15.9	15.7	34.6	34.5	34.6
(2)	-	-	mBART (black-box)	**20.8**	**21.1***	**21.2***	**21.2***	21.4*	21.2*	**15.9**	**15.9**	**16.1**	**33.9***	**33.4***	**33.0***
(3)	Word + Sentence	JaBERT + mBART		20.5	20.5	20.7	21.1	21.5*	21.4*	14.8*	14.8*	15.0*	32.4*	32.1*	31.6*
(4)	Word + Sentence	JaBERT + M2M-100		20.2*	20.4	20.2*	**21.2**	21.4*	21.5*	15.3	15.3	14.7*	32.1*	31.6*	31.3*
(5)	Word + Sentence	JaBERT + Denoiser		20.7	20.8	20.8	**21.2**	**21.7***	**21.7***	15.5	15.5	15.6	33.0*	32.4*	32.1*
(6)	Word + Sentence	mBERT + mBART		20.6	20.5	20.9	21.0	21.3*	21.5*	14.5*	14.7*	15.2	32.3*	32.2*	31.5*
(7)	Word + Sentence	mBERT + M2M-100		20.5	20.6	20.7	21.1	21.2	21.5*	15.3	15.2*	15.0*	32.3*	31.9*	31.5*
(8)	Word + Sentence	mBERT + Denoiser		**20.8**	20.8	20.8	21.0	21.2	21.6*	15.3	15.4	15.4	33.1*	32.4*	32.0*
(9)	-	-	MT (glass-box)	21.1*	21.2*	21.3*	20.9	21.2*	21.0	15.9	**15.9**	15.7	**34.7**	**34.3**	**34.4**
(10)	Word + Sentence	JaBERT + mBART		**21.2***	21.2*	21.3*	21.7*	21.9*	21.7*	15.8	15.6	15.6	34.3	34.2	34.0*
(11)	Word + Sentence	JaBERT + M2M-100		**21.2***	**21.3***	21.1	**21.8***	**22.2***	21.9*	16.0	15.8	15.5	34.2	34.2	34.0*
(12)	Word + Sentence	JaBERT + Denoiser		21.0	**21.3***	21.2*	21.5*	22.0*	21.8*	**16.2**	15.8	15.7	34.4	**34.3**	34.2
(13)	Word + Sentence	mBERT + mBART		**21.2***	21.2*	**21.6***	21.6*	21.8*	21.9*	15.7	15.5	15.7	34.4	34.2	33.9*
(14)	Word + Sentence	mBERT + M2M-100		**21.2***	21.2*	21.4*	**21.8***	21.9*	**22.1***	16.0	15.7	15.6	34.2	34.2	33.8*
(15)	Word + Sentence	mBERT + Denoiser		21.1*	**21.3***	21.4*	21.5*	21.7*	**22.1***	15.8	15.6	**15.9**	34.5	34.2	34.0*
(16)	-	-	Oracle	**26.0**	**27.9**	**29.8**	25.3	26.8	28.2	20.2	22.0	**23.8**	**40.1**	**41.5**	**42.9**
(17)	Word + Sentence	JaBERT + mBART		25.8	27.4	29.0	25.8	27.2	28.5	20.5	21.6	23.1	38.6	38.6	40.7
(18)	Word + Sentence	JaBERT + M2M-100		25.9	27.5	29.1	26.1	**27.6**	28.8	20.7	22.0	23.5	38.6	39.5	40.7
(19)	Word + Sentence	JaBERT + Denoiser		25.8	27.4	28.9	26.1	27.5	28.7	**20.9**	21.9	23.5	38.7	39.7	40.7
(20)	Word + Sentence	mBERT + mBART		25.7	27.5	29.2	25.9	27.1	28.6	20.1	21.6	23.0	38.5	39.6	40.6
(21)	Word + Sentence	mBERT + M2M-100		25.9	27.7	29.4	**26.3**	27.5	**28.9**	20.5	**22.1**	23.4	38.4	39.4	40.5
(22)	Word + Sentence	mBERT + Denoiser		25.8	27.5	29.3	26.2	27.5	28.8	20.6	22.0	23.4	38.6	39.6	40.7

Table 2: BLEU scores (k: number of paraphrases per word and sentence level respectively, **bold**: the highest BLEU score of each reranking result by column, *: statistically significant difference ($p < 0.05$) over the baseline method in the first row, underline: improvement over the component word-level paraphrasing method.)

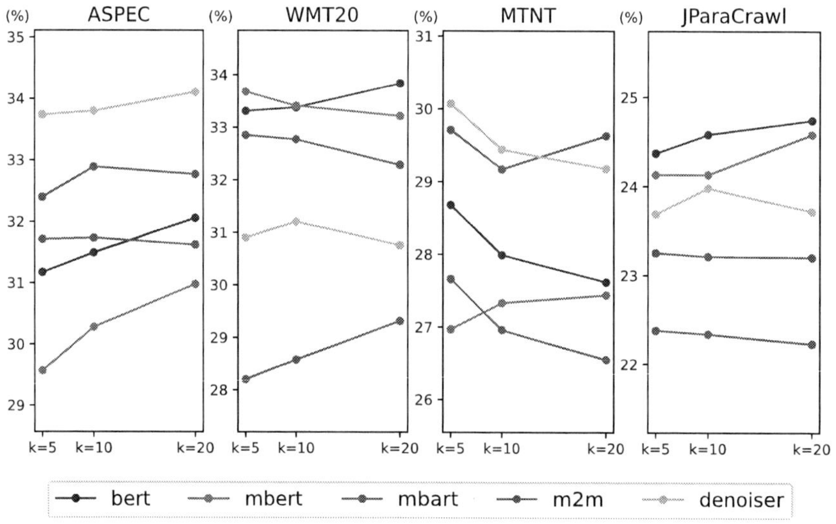

Figure 4: Percentage of candidate translations for paraphrases that have an increased sentence-level BLEU score compared to the translation for the original sentence. (k: number of paraphrases)

5 Conclusion

In this study, to mitigate the domain mismatch between the domains of the input sentence and the training data of the target MT system, we proposed a framework that combines paraphrase generation and reranking. In particular, the combination of word-level paraphrase generation and glass-box reranking consistently improved translation quality in the two specific domains most significantly.

Our future work will focus on improving reranking and filtering word-level paraphrases to further improve performance.

Acknowledgments

We would like to thank the reviewers for their insightful comments and suggestions. This work was supported by JST, ACT-X Grant Number JPMJAX1907. These research results were obtained from the commissioned research (No.22501) by National Institute of Information and Communications Technology (NICT), Japan.

References

Barrault, L., Biesialska, M., Bojar, O., Costa-jussà, M. R., Federmann, C., Graham, Y., Grundkiewicz, R., Haddow, B., Huck, M., Joanis, E., Kocmi, T., Koehn, P., Lo, C.-k., Ljubešić, N., Monz, C., Morishita, M., Nagata, M., Nakazawa, T., Pal, S., Post, M., and Zampieri, M. (2020). Findings of the 2020 Conference on Machine Translation. In *Proceedings of the Fifth Conference on Machine Translation*, pages 1–55.

Bojanowski, P., Grave, E., Joulin, A., and Mikolov, T. (2017). Enriching Word Vectors with Subword Information. *Transactions of the Association for Computational Linguistics*, 5:135–146.

Chu, C. and Wang, R. (2018). A Survey of Domain Adaptation for Neural Machine Translation. In *Proceedings of the 27th International Conference on Computational Linguistics*, pages 1304–1319.

Devlin, J., Chang, M.-W., Lee, K., and Toutanova, K. (2019). BERT: Pre-training of Deep Bidirectional Transformers for Language Understanding. In *Proceedings of the 2019 Conference of the North American Chapter of the Association for Computational Linguistics: Human Language Technologies*, pages 4171–4186.

Evans, R. J. (2011). Comparing Methods for the Syntactic Simplification of Sentences in Information Extraction. *Literary and Linguistic Computing*, 26(4):371–388.

Fan, A., Bhosale, S., Schwenk, H., Ma, Z., El-Kishky, A., Goyal, S., Baines, M., Celebi, O., Wenzek, G., Chaudhary, V., Goyal, N., Birch, T., Liptchinsky, V., Edunov, S., Grave, E., Auli, M., and Joulin, A. (2021). Beyond English-Centric Multilingual Machine Translation. *Journal of Machine Learning Research*, 22(1):4839–4886.

Kiyono, S., Ito, T., Konno, R., Morishita, M., and Suzuki, J. (2020). Tohoku-AIP-NTT at WMT 2020 news translation task. In *Proceedings of the Fifth Conference on Machine Translation*, pages 145–155.

Koehn, P. and Knowles, R. (2017). Six Challenges for Neural Machine Translation. In *Proceedings of the First Workshop on Neural Machine Translation*, pages 28–39.

Kudo, T. (2018). Subword Regularization: Improving Neural Network Translation Models with Multiple Subword Candidates. In *Proceedings of the 56th Annual Meeting of the Association for Computational Linguistics (Volume 1: Long Papers)*, pages 66–75.

Kudo, T. and Richardson, J. (2018). SentencePiece: A simple and language independent subword tokenizer and detokenizer for Neural Text Processing. In *Proceedings of the 2018 Conference on Empirical Methods in Natural Language Processing: System Demonstrations*, pages 66–71.

Li, X., Michel, P., Anastasopoulos, A., Belinkov, Y., Durrani, N., Firat, O., Koehn, P., Neubig, G., Pino, J., and Sajjad, H. (2019). Findings of the first shared task on machine translation robustness. In *Proceedings of the Fourth Conference on Machine Translation (Volume 2: Shared Task Papers, Day 1)*, pages 91–102.

Marie, B. and Fujita, A. (2018). A Smorgasbord of Features to Combine Phrase-Based and Neural Machine Translation. In *Proceedings of the 13th Conference of the Association for Machine Translation in the Americas*, pages 111–124.

Mehta, S., Azarnoush, B., Chen, B., Saluja, A., Misra, V., Bihani, B., and Kumar, R. (2020). Simplify-Then-Translate: Automatic Preprocessing for Black-Box Translation. In *Proceedings of the AAAI Conference on Artificial Intelligence*, pages 8488–8495.

Miyata, R. and Fujita, A. (2017). Dissecting Human Pre-Editing toward Better Use of Off-the-Shelf Machine Translation Systems. In *Proceedings of the 20th Annual Conference of the European Association for Machine Translation*, pages 54–59.

Miyata, R. and Fujita, A. (2021). Understanding Pre-Editing for Black-Box Neural Machine Translation. In *Proceedings of the 16th Conference of the European Chapter of the Association for Computational Linguistics*, pages 1539–1550.

Morishita, M., Chousa, K., Suzuki, J., and Nagata, M. (2022). JParaCrawl v3.0: A large-scale English-Japanese parallel corpus. In *Proceedings of the Thirteenth Language Resources and Evaluation Conference*, pages 6704–6710.

Nakazawa, T., Yaguchi, M., Uchimoto, K., Utiyama, M., Sumita, E., Kurohashi, S., and Isahara, H. (2016). ASPEC: Asian Scientific Paper Excerpt Corpus. In *Proceedings of the Tenth International Conference on Language Resources and Evaluation*, pages 2204–2208.

Ott, M., Edunov, S., Baevski, A., Fan, A., Gross, S., Ng, N., Grangier, D., and Auli, M. (2019). fairseq: A Fast, Extensible Toolkit for Sequence Modeling. In *Proceedings of the 2019 Conference of the North American Chapter of the Association for Computational Linguistics (Demonstrations)*, pages 48–53.

Papineni, K., Roukos, S., Ward, T., and Zhu, W.-J. (2002). BLEU: a Method for Automatic Evaluation of Machine Translation. In *Proceedings of the 40th Annual Meeting of the Association for Computational Linguistics*, pages 311–318.

Post, M. (2018). A Call for Clarity in Reporting BLEU Scores. In *Proceedings of the Third Conference on Machine Translation*, pages 186–191.

Siddharthan, A., Nenkova, A., and McKeown, K. (2004). Syntactic Simplification for Improving Content Selection in Multi-Document Summarization. In *Proceedings of the 20th International Conference on Computational Linguistics*, pages 896–902.

Štajner, S. and Popović, M. (2016). Can Text Simplification Help Machine Translation? In *Proceedings of the 19th Annual Conference of the European Association for Machine Translation*, pages 230–242.

Štajner, S. and Popović, M. (2018). Improving Machine Translation of English Relative Clauses with Automatic Text Simplification. In *Proceedings of the 1st Workshop on Automatic Text Adaptation*, pages 39–48.

Tang, Y., Tran, C., Li, X., Chen, P., Goyal, N., Chaudhary, V., Gu, J., and Fan, A. (2020). Multilingual Translation with Extensible Multilingual Pretraining and Finetuning. *CoRR*, abs/2008.00401.

Thompson, B. and Post, M. (2020a). Automatic machine translation evaluation in many languages via zero-shot paraphrasing. In *Proceedings of the 2020 Conference on Empirical Methods in Natural Language Processing (EMNLP)*, pages 90–121.

Thompson, B. and Post, M. (2020b). Paraphrase generation as zero-shot multilingual translation: Disentangling semantic similarity from lexical and syntactic diversity. In *Proceedings of the Fifth Conference on Machine Translation*, pages 561–570.

Vaswani, A., Shazeer, N., Parmar, N., Uszkoreit, J., Jones, L., Gomez, A. N., Kaiser, Ł., and Polosukhin, I. (2017). Attention is All you Need. In *Advances in Neural Information Processing Systems*, pages 5998–6008.

Wieting, J. and Gimpel, K. (2018). ParaNMT-50M: Pushing the Limits of Paraphrastic Sentence Embeddings with Millions of Machine Translations. In *Proceedings of the 56th Annual Meeting of the Association for Computational Linguistics (Volume 1: Long Papers)*, pages 451–462.

BITS-P at WAT 2023: Improving Indic Language Multimodal Translation by Image Augmentation using Diffusion Models

Amulya Ratna Dash[†*] p20200105@pilani.bits-pilani.ac.in
Hrithik Raj Gupta[†] f20190995@pilani.bits-pilani.ac.in
Yashvardhan Sharma[†] yash@pilani.bits-pilani.ac.in
†BITS Pilani, Pilani, Rajasthan, India
*IQVIA, Bangalore, Karnataka, India

Abstract

This paper describes the proposed system for mutlimodal machine translation. We have participated in multimodal translation tasks for English into three Indic languages: Hindi, Bengali, and Malayalam. We leverage the inherent richness of multimodal data to bridge the gap of ambiguity in translation. We fine-tuned the 'No Language Left Behind' (NLLB) machine translation model for multimodal translation, further enhancing the model accuracy by image data augmentation using latent diffusion. Our submission achieves the best BLEU score for English-Hindi, English-Bengali, and English-Malayalam language pairs for both Evaluation and Challenge test sets.

1 Introduction

Machine Translation (MT) is the NLP task of translation between language pairs. Multimodal Machine Translation (MMT) is the translation process that utilizes information from multiple modalities, not just text. The most popular approach is to use extra visual context in addition to the source text input. The visual context is presented in the form of images that are relevant to the text to be translated and may help in cases of ambiguity.

In 10th Workshop on Asian Translation (WAT 2023), we investigate Multimodal Machine Translation for English to Hindi, Bengali, and Malayalam languages by fine-tuning the 'No Language Left Behind' (NLLB) pre-trained machine translation model by Costa-jussà et al. (2022) and using image data augmentation techniques. Figure 1 shows an example where the visual context of an image helps generate accurate machine-translated text.

The rest of the paper is organized as follows: Section 2 presents the review of related works. The data and system are briefly described in Section 3. Section 4 reports the results, followed by the future scope and conclusion in Section 5.

2 Related Work

In the literature survey, there are some multimodal machine translation works that take both text and image as input, and learn joint multimodal representations from images and text (Specia et al., 2016). Huang et al. (2016) incorporated an object detection system, extracting local and global image features as additional inputs to the encoder and decoder. Lin et al. (2020) utilized

Proceedings of the 10th Workshop on Asian Translation, pages 41–45
September 4, 2023, Macau SAR, China

Image caption: A large pipe extending from the wall of the court.
Hindi translation: कोर्ट की दीवार से निकली हुई एक बडी पाइप
Bengali translation: কোর্টের দেয়াল থেকে প্রসারিত একটি বৃহত্ পাইপ।
Malayalam translation: കോർട്ടിന്റെ മതിലിൽ നിന്ന് നീളുന്ന ഒരു വലിയ പൈപ്പ്.

Figure 1: Example of Multimodal translation

Dynamic Context-guided Capsule Network (DCCN) for iterative extraction of related visual features. Most of them investigated multimodal MT for high-resource European languages. There are only a few works for Indic languages.

Dutta Chowdhury et al. (2018) who employed synthetic data for training and used multimodal, attention-based MT incorporating visual features into the encoder and decoder (Calixto and Liu, 2017). Su et al. (2019) further demonstrated the advantage of jointly learning text-image interaction rather than modeling them separately using attentional networks.

Parida et al. (2019) proposed a subset of the Visual Genome dataset (Krishna et al., 2017) for multimodal translation between English and Hindi, a less explored language pair in this context. Parida et al. (2021) used the Bengali Visual Genome (Sen et al., 2022) and adopted the ViTA (Gupta et al., 2021) approach, with mBART (Liu et al., 2020) for encoding English sentences with object tags and decoding Bengali translations.

Our current work builds upon these foundations, introducing a novel approach using NLLB and Stable Diffusion (Rombach et al., 2022) to multimodal translation, with a specific focus on the English to Hindi, Bengali, and Malayalam language pairs.

3 System Overview

In this section, we describe the dataset, data augmentation technique, and model approach for the proposed system we use for the multimodal translation task.

3.1 Dataset Description

The primary datasets utilized for training are the Hindi Visual Genome (HVG), the Bengali Visual Genome (BVG), and the Malayalam Visual Genome (MVG). The HVG dataset comprises of around 29K parallel English-Hindi sentence pairs, each associated with an image. Each data point in the multimodal dataset contains an image alongside a textual description of a certain rectangular portion of the image, delineated by provided coordinates. The task is to translate these descriptions using contextual support from the images.

The datasets also contain three test sets apart from the training set: a development test set (D-Test), an evaluation test set (E-Test), and a challenge test set (C-Test). The BVG and MVG datasets are structured identically to HVG, with the same images and image captions, but the captions are translated into Bengali and Malayalam, respectively.

We augmented the training data by using Stable Diffusion (v. 1.5)[1] to generate synthetic

[1]https://huggingface.co/runwayml/stable-diffusion-v1-5

images based on the English image captions. This technique doubled the image data available for each sentence in the training dataset, providing us with two images for each sentence. We prepared two set of training data, one with 26K data points (Visual Genome) and the other which includes additional 26K data points based on synthetic images. Our final training dataset consists of around 58K unique data points.

3.2 Model Description

DETR (DEtection TRansformer) (Carion et al., 2020) is a transformer-based object detection model that performs end-to-end object detection by directly outputting object detections as sets, eliminating the need for traditional region proposal methods. To extract the image features, we used the DETR object detection system with a ResNet-50 backbone[2]. This allowed us to identify the objects contained within each image. We appended the sentences with a comma-separated list of detected objects preceded by '##' to ensure a clear demarcation between the sentence and the object list.

We fine-tuned the NLLB-200 model[3] for each language with randomly shuffled training dataset, using the D-Test set of our datasets as the validation dataset with 998 data points. We fine-tuned the model for Hindi and Bengali for 100 epochs, while the Malayalam model was fine-tuned for 70 epochs.

The fine-tuning was accomplished utilizing an NVIDIA A100 GPU, and the following training hyperparameters were used: learning rate: 2e-05, batch size: 32, Optimizer: Adam, configured with β_1 = 0.9, β_2 = 0.999, and ϵ = 1e-08.4, and learning rate scheduling: linear.

We trained two models for Hindi language, one with original training dataset and the other with data augmentation for comparative evaluation. Both the models used same hyperparameters and trained for 100 epochs.

4 Experimental Results

Our model achieves promising results during the automated evaluation[4]. To evaluate our model, we used two test sets: i) Evaluation set (E-Test) with 1595 sentences, and ii) Challenge set (C-Test) with 1400 sentences. We test our model on both of these test sets and present the results in Table 1, Table 2, and Table 3 for English-Bengali, English-Hindi, and English-Malayalam tasks, respectively. We use BLEU and RIBES as evaluation metrics.

The English-Hindi multimodal machine translation model trained with additional synthetic image data achieves 52.10 and 45 BLEU score on C-Test and E-Test, while the baseline model trained only on Hindi Visual Genome data achieves 51.20 and 44.90 BLEU score on C-Test and E-Test respectively. The data augmentation technique improved the BLEU score by +0.9 on Challenge set (C-Test).

[2]https://huggingface.co/facebook/detr-resnet-50
[3]https://huggingface.co/facebook/nllb-200-distilled-1.3B
[4]https://lotus.kuee.kyoto-u.ac.jp/WAT/evaluation/index.html

Test			
Team	**Data ID**	**BLEU**	**RIBES**
BITS-P	7123	**50.60**	**0.814207**
Best-Comp	6743	43.90	0.780669
Challenge Test			
Team	**Data ID**	**BLEU**	**RIBES**
BITS-P	7122	**48.70**	**0.831946**
Best-Comp	7108	30.50	0.690706

Table 1: Results for EN-BN multimodal translation task

Test			
Team	**Data ID**	**BLEU**	**RIBES**
BITS-P	7125	**45.00**	**0.829320**
Best-Comp	6428	44.64	0.823319
Challenge Test			
Team	**Data ID**	**BLEU**	**RIBES**
BITS-P	7124	**52.10**	0.853388
Best-Comp	6430	51.60	**0.859645**

Table 2: Results for EN-HI multimodal translation task

Test			
Team	**Data ID**	**BLEU**	**RIBES**
BITS-P	7127	**51.90**	**0.799683**
Best-Comp	6936	41.00	0.705349
Challenge Test			
Team	**Data ID**	**BLEU**	**RIBES**
BITS-P	7126	**42.20**	**0.759248**
Best-Comp	6937	20.40	0.533737

Table 3: Results for EN-ML multimodal translation task

5 Conclusion

In this paper, we described our multimodal machine translation system. Our system scored 50.60 and 48.70 BLEU points for Bengali; 45.00 and 52.10 BLEU points for Hindi, and 51.90 and 42.20 BLEU points for Malayalam for Evaluation and Challenge test sets, respectively. The data augmentation strategy of using synthetic images generated by diffusion models improved the system by +0.9 BLEU score. In the future, we would further explore data augmentation approaches for text data using image captioning frameworks.

References

Calixto, I. and Liu, Q. (2017). Incorporating global visual features into attention-based neural machine translation. In *Proceedings of the 2017 Conference on Empirical Methods in Natural Language Processing*, pages 992–1003, Copenhagen, Denmark. Association for Computational Linguistics.

Carion, N., Massa, F., Synnaeve, G., Usunier, N., Kirillov, A., and Zagoruyko, S. (2020). End-to-end object detection with transformers. In *European conference on computer vision*, pages 213–229. Springer.

Costa-jussà, M. R., Cross, J., Çelebi, O., Elbayad, M., Heafield, K., Heffernan, K., Kalbassi, E., Lam, J., Licht, D., Maillard, J., et al. (2022). No language left behind: Scaling human-centered machine translation. *arXiv preprint arXiv:2207.04672*.

Dutta Chowdhury, K., Hasanuzzaman, M., and Liu, Q. (2018). Multimodal neural machine translation for low-resource language pairs using synthetic data. In *Proceedings of the Workshop on Deep Learning Approaches for Low-Resource NLP*, pages 33–42, Melbourne. Association for Computational Linguistics.

Gupta, K., Gautam, D., and Mamidi, R. (2021). ViTA: Visual-linguistic translation by aligning object tags. In *Proceedings of the 8th Workshop on Asian Translation (WAT2021)*, pages 166–173, Online. Association for Computational Linguistics.

Huang, P.-Y., Liu, F., Shiang, S.-R., Oh, J., and Dyer, C. (2016). Attention-based multimodal neural machine translation. In *Proceedings of the First Conference on Machine Translation: Volume 2, Shared Task Papers*, pages 639–645, Berlin, Germany. Association for Computational Linguistics.

Krishna, R., Zhu, Y., Groth, O., Johnson, J., Hata, K., Kravitz, J., Chen, S., Kalantidis, Y., Li, L.-J., Shamma, D. A., et al. (2017). Visual genome: Connecting language and vision using crowdsourced dense image annotations. *International journal of computer vision*, 123:32–73.

Lin, H., Meng, F., Su, J., Yin, Y., Yang, Z., Ge, Y., Zhou, J., and Luo, J. (2020). Dynamic context-guided capsule network for multimodal machine translation. In *Proceedings of the 28th ACM International Conference on Multimedia*, MM '20, page 1320–1329, New York, NY, USA. Association for Computing Machinery.

Liu, Y., Gu, J., Goyal, N., Li, X., Edunov, S., Ghazvininejad, M., Lewis, M., and Zettlemoyer, L. (2020). Multilingual denoising pre-training for neural machine translation. *Transactions of the Association for Computational Linguistics*, 8:726–742.

Parida, S., Bojar, O., and Dash, S. R. (2019). Hindi Visual Genome: A Dataset for Multimodal English-to-Hindi Machine Translation. *Computación y Sistemas*, 23(4):1499–1505. Presented at CICLing 2019, La Rochelle, France.

Parida, S., Panda, S., Biswal, S. P., Kotwal, K., Sen, A., Dash, S. R., and Motlicek, P. (2021). Multimodal neural machine translation system for English to Bengali. In *Proceedings of the First Workshop on Multimodal Machine Translation for Low Resource Languages (MMTLRL 2021)*, pages 31–39, Online (Virtual Mode). INCOMA Ltd.

Rombach, R., Blattmann, A., Lorenz, D., Esser, P., and Ommer, B. (2022). High-resolution image synthesis with latent diffusion models. In *Proceedings of the IEEE/CVF conference on computer vision and pattern recognition*, pages 10684–10695.

Sen, A., Parida, S., Kotwal, K., Panda, S., Bojar, O., and Dash, S. R. (2022). Bengali visual genome: A multimodal dataset for machine translation and image captioning. In *Intelligent Data Engineering and Analytics*, pages 63–70. Springer.

Specia, L., Frank, S., Sima'an, K., and Elliott, D. (2016). A shared task on multimodal machine translation and crosslingual image description. In *Proceedings of the First Conference on Machine Translation: Volume 2, Shared Task Papers*, pages 543–553, Berlin, Germany. Association for Computational Linguistics.

Su, Y., Fan, K., Bach, N., Kuo, C.-C. J., and Huang, F. (2019). Unsupervised multi-modal neural machine translation. In *Proceedings of the IEEE/CVF Conference on Computer Vision and Pattern Recognition*, pages 10482–10491.

OdiaGenAI's Participation at WAT2023

Sk Shahid Silicon Institute of Technology, Bhubaneswar, India
Guneet Singh Kohli Thapar Institute of Engineering & Technology, India
Sambit Sekhar Odia Generative AI, Bhubaneswar, India
Debasish Dhal NISER, Bhubaneswar, India
Adit Sharma Jaypee Institute of Information Technology, Noida, India
Shubhendra Kushwaha ITER, Siksha 'O'Anusandhan, Bhubaneswar, India
Shantipriya Parida Silo AI, Helsinki, Finland
Stig-Arne Grönroos Silo AI, Helsinki, Finland
Satya Ranjan Dash KIIT University, Bhubaneswar, India

Abstract

This paper offers an in-depth overview of the team "ODIAGEN's" translation system submitted to the Workshop on Asian Translation (WAT2023). Our focus lies in the domain of Indic Multimodal tasks, specifically targeting English to Hindi, English to Malayalam, and English to Bengali translations. The system uses a state-of-the-art Transformer-based architecture, specifically the NLLB-200 model, fine-tuned with language-specific Visual Genome Datasets. With this robust system, we were able to manage both text-to-text and multimodal translations, demonstrating versatility in handling different translation modes.

Our results showcase strong performance across the board, with particularly promising results in the Hindi and Bengali translation tasks. A noteworthy achievement of our system lies in its stellar performance across all text-to-text translation tasks. In the categories of English to Hindi, English to Bengali, and English to Malayalam translations, our system claimed the top positions for both the evaluation and challenge sets.

This system not only advances our understanding of the challenges and nuances of Indic language translation but also opens avenues for future research to enhance translation accuracy and performance.

1 Introduction

Machine translation (MT) is a well-established field within Natural Language Processing (NLP) that focuses on developing computer software to automatically translate text or speech between different languages. While significant progress has been made in achieving human-level translation for high-resource languages, challenges still remain, especially for low-resource languages (Popel et al., 2020; Costa-jussà et al., 2022). Additionally, recent research has explored the effective integration of other modalities, such as images, into the machine translation process.

Proceedings of the 10th Workshop on Asian Translation, pages 46–52
September 4, 2023, Macau SAR, China

The WAT is an open evaluation campaign focusing on Asian languages since 2013 (Nakazawa et al., 2020, 2022). The multimodal translation tasks in WAT2023 consist of image caption translation, in which the input is a descriptive source language caption together with the image it describes, while the output is a target language caption. The multimodal input enables the use of image context to disambiguate source words with multiple senses.

In this system description paper, we (team "ODIAGEN") explains our approach for the tasks (including the sub-tasks) we participated in:

Task 1: English→Hindi (EN-HI) Multimodal Translation

- EN-HI text-only translation
- EN-HI multimodal translation

Task 2: English→Malayalam (EN-ML) Multimodal Translation

- EN-ML text-only translation
- EN-ML multimodal translation

Task 3: English→Bengali (EN-BN) Multimodal Translation

- EN-BN text-only translation
- EN-BN multimodal translation

2 Datasets

We used the datasets specified by the organizer for the related tasks without any additional synthetic data.

Task 1: English→Hindi Multimodal Translation For this task, the organizers provided HindiVisualGenome 1.1 (Parida et al., 2019)[1] dataset (HVG for short). The training part consists of 29k English and Hindi short captions of rectangular areas in photos of various scenes and it is complemented by three test sets: development (D-Test), evaluation (E-Test) and challenge test set (C-Test). Our WAT submissions were for E-Test (denoted "EV" in WAT official tables) and C-Test (denoted "CH" in WAT tables).

The statistics of the datasets are shown in Table 1.

Task 2: English→Malayalam Multimodal Translation For this task, the organizers provided MalayalamVisualGenome 1.0 dataset[2] (MVG for short). MVG is an extension of the HVG dataset for supporting Malayalam, which belongs to the Dravidian language family (Kumar et al., 2017). The dataset size and images are the same as HVG. While HVG contains bilingual English–Hindi segments, MVG contains bilingual English–Malayalam segments, with the English, shared across HVG and MVG, see Table 1.

Task 3: English→Bengali Multimodal Translation For this task, the organizers provided BengaliVisualGenome 1.0 dataset[3] (BVG for short). BVG is an extension of the HVG dataset for supporting Bengali. The dataset size and images are the same as HVG, and MVG, see Table 1.

[1] `https://lindat.mff.cuni.cz/repository/xmlui/handle/11234/1-3267`
[2] `https://lindat.mff.cuni.cz/repository/xmlui/handle/11234/1-3533`
[3] `http://hdl.handle.net/11234/1-3722`

Set	Sentences	Tokens			
		English	Hindi	Malayalam	Bengali
Train	28930	143164	145448	107126	113978
D-Test	998	4922	4978	3619	3936
E-Test	1595	7853	7852	5689	6408
C-Test	1400	8186	8639	6044	6657

Table 1: Statistics of our data used in the English→Hindi, English→Malayalam, and English→Bengali task: the number of sentences and tokens.

3 Experimental Details

This section describes the experimental details of the tasks we participated in.

3.1 EN-HI, EN-ML, EN-BN text-only translation

For EN–HI, EN-BN, and EN–ML text-only (E-Test and C-Test) translation, the study fine-tunes the pre-trained NLLB-200 model (NLLB Team et al., 2022), which has been fine-tuned utilizing HVG, BVG, MVG Datasets; aiming to develop a high-quality machine translation system. The NLLB-200 model, a distilled version with 600 million parameters, is used as the base model. It's a Seq2Seq (Sequence-to-Sequence) model, a type of model designed to convert sequences from one domain (like sentences in one language) to sequences in another domain (like sentences in another language). We leverage the Hugging Face's transformers library, specifically using the `AutoModelForSeq2SeqLM` class for the model architecture as shown in Figure 1.

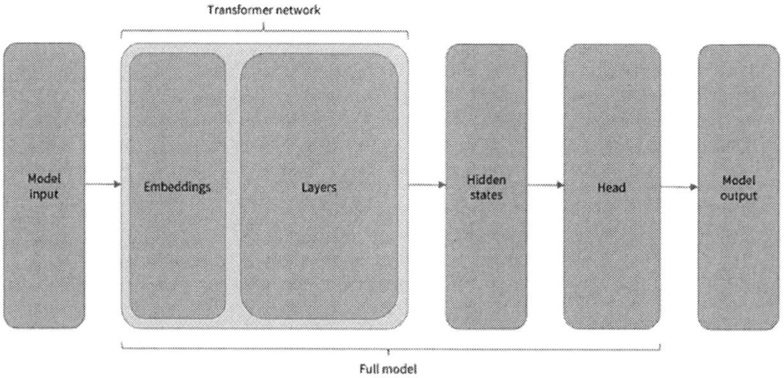

Figure 1: Model Architechture

The pipeline shown in Figure 2 includes several distinct steps:

- **Preprocessing**: The raw text data, which consists of source language sentences and their corresponding target translations, undergoes a preprocessing step. Here, each sentence in both languages is tokenized using a fast tokenizer that leverages **Byte-Pair Encoding (BPE)** (Sennrich et al., 2016). For each sentence, the tokenizer returns an input-ids array, which is a numerical representation of the tokenized sentence, additionally, an attention-mask array is created to indicate the positions of actual tokens. This step results in preprocessed model inputs that include input ids and attention-mask for both source (English) and target (HI/BN/ML) languages.

- **Model Fine-tuning**: The preprocessed inputs are then fed into the NLLB-200 model for training. Given the supervised nature of the task, the model learns to map the source input tokens to the corresponding target tokens. During this process, the model adjusts its internal parameters to minimize the difference between its predictions and the actual target sentences (the labels).

- **Post-processing**: After training, the model generates predictions (preds) for a given English input. These predictions are in the form of token ids, which are then decoded back into their corresponding target sentences using the `tokenizer.batch-decode` function. This decoding process converts the numeric predictions of the model back into human-readable text, ready for evaluation.

- **Evaluation**: Finally, the quality of the model's translations is evaluated using the **Bilingual Evaluation Understudy (BLEU)** score (Papineni et al., 2002). The BLEU score is a popular metric in machine translation that compares machine-generated translations to one or more human-generated reference translations. It provides a quantitative measure of translation quality, with higher scores indicating better performance.

Overall, this pipeline encapsulates the entire process from preprocessing to evaluation, offering a streamlined method for training and validating an English to Hindi/Bengali/Malayalam machine translation model.

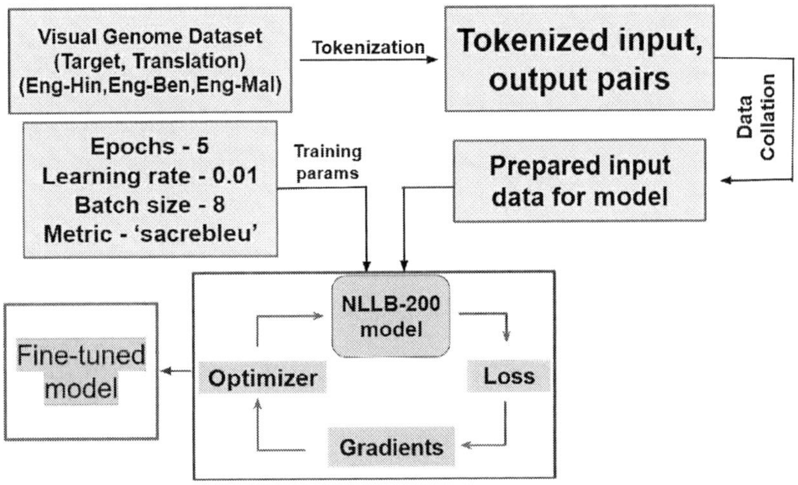

Figure 2: Fine-tuning of NLLB-200 pre-trained model with Visual Genome Dataset

3.2 EN-HI, EN-ML, EN-BN Multimodal translation

This section discusses the multimodal translation pipeline for EN-HI and EN-BN. For EN-HI multimodal (E-Test and CTest) translation, we used the object tags extracted from the HVG dataset images for image features and concatenated them with the text.

Similarly, For EN-BN (E-Test and C-Test) translation, we used object tags extracted from the BVG dataset.

We derive the extracted object tags using a pre-trained Faster RCNN with ResNet101-C4 backbone, which can recognize 80 object types that constitute the COCO Dataset (Lin et al., 2014). In the next step, we select the top 10 tags based on the confidence scores, and in case the object tags are less than 10, we select all the detected tags. The original input English instance is concatenated with a '##' as a separator followed by comma-separated detected tags. This formatted input loaded with visual context from the object tags is fed into the mBART Encoder for processing.

4 Results

We report the official automatic evaluation results of our models for all the participating tasks in Table 2 and sample outputs in Table 3.

Following the fine-tuning process, these models were used to infer translations on two distinct sets for each language: the evaluation set and the challenge set. The translation quality was evaluated using the BLEU (Bilingual Evaluation Understudy) score, and RIBES (Ranking by Incremental Bilingual Evaluation System) score.

For the English-to-Hindi model, a BLEU score of 44.60 was achieved on the evaluation set, while a score of 53.60 was obtained for the challenge set. These results highlight the model's strong performance and its capacity to handle more complex or unusual translation tasks.

In the case of the English-to-Bengali model, a BLEU score of 49.20 was reached on the evaluation set, with a slightly lower score of 47.80 on the challenge set. This indicates a robust overall performance and a commendable capability to handle nuanced translations specific to the Bengali language.

Lastly, for the English-to-Malayalam model, the system achieved a BLEU score of 46.60 on the evaluation set and 39.70 on the challenge set. Despite a slightly lower score on the challenge set, the model still demonstrates a respectable performance in translating English to Malayalam.

Translation Model	Translation Type	BLUE Score (Evaluation Set)	BLEU Score (Challenge Set)
English to Hindi	Text-to-Text	44.60	53.60
	Multimodal	41.60	42.80
English to Bengali	Text-to-Text	49.20	47.80
	Multimodal	42.40	30.50
English to Malayalam	Text-to-Text	46.60	39.70

Table 2: BLEU scores of the text-to-text and multimodal translation models on the evaluation and challenge sets, from the official leaderboard.

The lower BLEU score on the English to Malayalam translation task can be due to a lot of possible factors, one of which is Linguistic Complexity, as Malayalam is a Dravidian language known for its complex grammatical structures and a rich set of linguistic phenomena, which may not be easily captured by the model. This complexity can make the mapping from English to Malayalam challenging.

	MALAYALAM	HINDI	BENGALI
English-Sentence-1	silver car is parked	fine thin red hair	A stop light
Target-Original	സിൽവർ കാർ പാർക്ക് ചെയ്തു	सूक्ष्म पतले लाल बाल	একটি স্টপ লাইট
Target-Translated	വെള്ളി കാർ പാർക്ക് ചെയ്തിരിക്കുന്നു	ठीक पतले लाल बाल	একটি স্টপ আলো
Gloss	Silver car has been parked	Correct thin red hair	A stop light
Remarks (Comparison)	Translated version is more formal	Original version is better "Fine" mistranslated by our model.	Original version is more colloquial
English-Sentence-2	eye of the pumpkin	the cross is black	This is a person
Target-Original	മത്തങ്ങയുടെ കണ്ണ്	क्रॉस काला है	এটি একজন ব্যক্তি
Target-Translated	പമ്മിക്കിന്റെ കണ്ണ്	क्रॉस काला है	এটি একজন ব্যক্তি
Gloss	Pumpkin's eyes	The cross is black	This is a person
Remarks (Comparison)	Model doesn't translate "pumpkin", which is colloquial	Both are identical	Both are identical
English-Sentence-3	pen on the paper	date and time of photo	the bird is black
Target-Original	പേപ്പറിൽ പേന	फोटो की तारीख और समय	পাখিটি কালো
Target-Translated	പേപ്പറിൽ പേന	फोटो की तारीख और समय	পাখিটি কালো
Gloss	Pen on the paper	Date and time of photo	The bird is black
Remarks (Comparison)	Both are identical	Both are identical	Both are identical

Table 3: Comparison between original translations and our model's translations for English-Malayalam, English-Hindi and English-Bengali language pairs.

5 Conclusion

In this system description paper, we presented our system for three tasks in WAT2023: (a) English→Hindi, (b) English→Malayalam, and (c) English→Bengali Multimodal Translation. We released the code through Github for research[4].

These empirical results underscore the effectiveness of the methodology adopted for these machine translation models. Leveraging a fine-tuned NLLB-200 model with language-specific Visual Genome Datasets provides a robust solution to the machine translation task for the languages under study: Hindi, Bengali, and Malayalam. The results also pave the way for further enhancements and investigations in the realm of machine translation.

Acknowledgements

We are thankful to Silo AI, Helsinki, Finland, and Odia Generative AI, Bhubaneswar, India for the necessary support for participating in WAT2023.

References

Costa-jussà, M. R., Cross, J., Çelebi, O., Elbayad, M., Heafield, K., Heffernan, K., Kalbassi, E., Lam, J., Licht, D., Maillard, J., et al. (2022). No language left behind: Scaling human-centered machine translation. *arXiv e-prints*, pages arXiv–2207.

Kumar, A., Cotterell, R., Padró, L., and Oliver, A. (2017). Morphological analysis of the Dravidian language family. In *Proceedings of the 15th Conference of the European Chapter of the Association for Computational Linguistics: Volume 2, Short Papers*, pages 217–222.

[4]`https://github.com/shantipriyap/wat2023`

Lin, T.-Y., Maire, M., Belongie, S., Hays, J., Perona, P., Ramanan, D., Dollár, P., and Zitnick, C. L. (2014). Microsoft COCO: Common objects in context. In *European conference on computer vision*, pages 740–755. Springer.

Nakazawa, T., Mino, H., Goto, I., Dabre, R., Higashiyama, S., Parida, S., Kunchukuttan, A., Morishita, M., Bojar, O., Chu, C., Eriguchi, A., Abe, K., Oda, Y., and Kurohashi, S. (2022). Overview of the 9th workshop on Asian translation. In *Proceedings of the 9th Workshop on Asian Translation (WAT2022)*, Gyeongju, Republic of Korea. Association for Computational Linguistics.

Nakazawa, T., Nakayama, H., Ding, C., Dabre, R., Higashiyama, S., Mino, H., Goto, I., Pa, W. P., Kunchukuttan, A., Parida, S., et al. (2020). Overview of the 7th workshop on Asian translation. In *Proceedings of the 7th Workshop on Asian Translation*, pages 1–44.

NLLB Team, Costa-jussà, M. R., Cross, J., Çelebi, O., Elbayad, M., Heafield, K., Heffernan, K., Kalbassi, E., Lam, J., Licht, D., Maillard, J., Sun, A., Wang, S., Wenzek, G., Youngblood, A., Akula, B., Barrault, L., Gonzalez, G. M., Hansanti, P., Hoffman, J., Jarrett, S., Sadagopan, K. R., Rowe, D., Spruit, S., Tran, C., Andrews, P., Ayan, N. F., Bhosale, S., Edunov, S., Fan, A., Gao, C., Goswami, V., Guzmán, F., Koehn, P., Mourachko, A., Ropers, C., Saleem, S., Schwenk, H., and Wang, J. (2022). No language left behind: Scaling human-centered machine translation.

Papineni, K., Roukos, S., Ward, T., and Zhu, W.-J. (2002). Bleu: A method for automatic evaluation of machine translation. In *Proceedings of the 40th Annual Meeting on Association for Computational Linguistics*, ACL '02, page 311–318, USA. Association for Computational Linguistics.

Parida, S., Bojar, O., and Dash, S. R. (2019). Hindi visual genome: A dataset for multimodal English to Hindi machine translation. *Computación y Sistemas*, 23(4):1499–1505.

Popel, M., Tomkova, M., Tomek, J., Kaiser, Ł., Uszkoreit, J., Bojar, O., and Žabokrtský, Z. (2020). Transforming machine translation: a deep learning system reaches news translation quality comparable to human professionals. *Nature communications*, 11(1):1–15.

Sennrich, R., Haddow, B., and Birch, A. (2016). Neural machine translation of rare words with subword units.

Author Index